WITH **EMILIE BARNES** CO-AUTHOR OF
Eating Right!

D1558109

Casseroles

Meals in Minutes

*for Busy Women**

SUE GREGG

Eating Better Cookbooks

PUBLICATIONS BY SUE GREGG AND EMILIE BARNES

Eating Right! A Realistic Approach to a Healthy Lifestyle
    (Harvest House, 1987)

Eating Better with Sue, Video
    (Fabian Productions, 1988)

Sue Gregg (Eating Better Cookbooks)
    Main Dishes
    Soups & Muffins
    Casseroles
    Lunches & Snacks
    Breakfasts
    Desserts
    Holiday Menus
    The Creative Recipe Organizer
    The Eating Better Menu Planner
    Quantity Recipes
    Eating Better with Sue Cooking Course Workbook
    Eating Better with Sue Cooking Course Leader's Guide

Emilie Barnes (Harvest House)
    More Hours in My Day
    Survival for Busy Women
    The Creative Home Organizer
    The 15 Minute Organizer
    The Holiday Organizer
    Growing a Great Marriage
    Things Happen When Women Care
    The Daily Planner

Published and distributed by

EATING BETTER COOKBOOKS
8830 Glencoe Drive
Riverside, California 92503

Holy Bible: New International Version,
Copyright © by the New York International Bible Society.
Used by permission of Zondervan Bible Publishers.

DISCLAIMER

This cookbook is designed to provide information relating to the subject matter covered. It is sold with the understanding that the publisher and author are not engaged in rendering medical, nutritional, dietary, or other professional services. If expert assistance is required, the reader should seek the services of a competent medical professional.

This cookbook does not cover or reprint all of the information on the subject available to the author, publisher, or the reader. Research in the field of nutrition often seems conflicting, and when hyped by media and advertising, contradictory and confusing. You are urged to read all the available material, to inform yourself as much as possible about nutrition and food preparation, and then with the advice of competent professionals to tailor the information to your personal needs.

Health is not achieved through one shot schemes, potions, or pills. It is not acquired through diet alone. Anyone who decides to pursue it must expect to invest time, effort, and discipline. We are reminded, however, that even those who inherit or achieve even the best health do not live forever. "It is appointed to man once to die..." Therefore, the reader is urged not just to prepare for the immediate, but also to discover the Creator's eternal plan.

With every edition and printing of this cookbook every effort is made to make the information as accurate, complete, and up-to-date as possible. However, experience tells us that mistakes are inevitable in content, data caculations, and typography. This cookbook should be used only as a general guide and not as the ultimate source of information on food preparation and nutrition.

The purpose of this cookbook is to model and motivate, to educate and entertain. The author and the publisher, shall have neither liability nor responsibility to any person or entity with respect to any loss or damage caused, alleged to be caused, directly or indirectly by the information contained in this book.

If you do not wish to be bound by the above, you may return this book to the publisher for a full refund.

What others are saying...

I go all the way now with "Eating Better." My energy level has increased greatly! That's the best part, but another benefit has been a 20 lb. weight loss!

Betty, Jenison, Michigan

Your recipes have really encouraged my cooking and my husband is very pleased. Happy husband means a happy wife!

Christa, San Bernardino, California

*I purchased a set of cookbooks and **Eating Right!** It's been a great week. Even my husband and daughter have liked everything I've made. It's easy and it makes sense. Thank you!*

Marie, Moreno Valley, California

We enjoy all your recipes. Since we've started using the Eating Better Cookbooks exclusively, I've lost 15 lbs. And without even trying!

Kristine, San Diego, California

I love the cookbooks and menu planner! I've been converting recipes and using various health cookbooks for years, but these are far superior! Thanks!

Sara, Pasadena, Texas

Our weekly food budget has decreased from $125 to $70. I can't thank you enough.

Sheila, Ontario, Canada

I entered your Oatbran Muffin recipe in the Los Angeles County Fair and won 2nd place!

Jane Kayser, Moreno Valley, California

We've had lots of allergy problems and have been on rotation diets, vegetarian diets, combination diets, no dairy diets... Cooking became a trial to be put off as long as possible. Your books are sensible... We have only begun, but so far it is all I'd hoped for and more.

Sherry, Bartlesville, Oklahoma

*I've been using the **Eating Better Cookbooks** for 1 1/2 years. After 10 years of marriage, what a blessing to hear "This is good! This is really good!" Recipe after recipe! Praise God!*

Kathe Moran, Sacramento, California

Contents

Recipe list

Cook's Prayer

O LORD, Maker of Heaven and Earth's Land,
* You made the wheat, the germ, the bran--*
*   Nutrient and fiber-rich for the strength of man.*
* Cheeses 'n chicken, fish, beef, 'n dairy--*
*   A little goes a long way to refresh the weary.*

* And vegetables countless--nutrient-packed treasure.*
* Succulent fruits for dessert: What delightful pleasure!*
* And nuts 'n seeds for essential fats in good measure.*

* Beans 'n peas for more protein and fiber, please!*
* With plenteous water to cook them,*
*   Poured out by the Lord of Seas.*
*   What great gifts, these!*
* Your store of food in all colors, shapes, and sizes*
* Are ever full of nutrient and taste surprises!*

* Honey dripping from the comb,*
*   of this sweet offering could be written a tome.*
* Spices and herbs to jazz up flavor,*
* Even salt and egg yolks we count not totally*
*   out of your favor!*

Now LORD, our Lord,
* Help us to put your bounty together*
*   In balance and wholeness that we might eat better,*
*   For bodies stronger,*
*   And minds sharper;*
*   For spirits assisted,*
*   And service enlisted,*
*   To sow the seed; to reap the harvest*
*   From the nearest land to the farthest.*

Thanks be to you, O God, Our LORD,
*   For food from your hand*
*   We can afford!*
*   Please help us to share it with our brothers*
*   and sisters,*
*   And to serve it to our dear children.*
*   As your Son broke 5 loaves and 2 fish*
*   to feed more than 5,000,*
*   So break us, LORD,*
*   to feed more than 4 billion.*

Foreword

I received a call from a busy working woman soon after giving a seminar in Southern California. She related a story I must share with you.

After purchasing your **Main Dishes** *I decided to try the eating right recipes out on my own family. It was a delight to me how easy they were put together and loved by all.*

One Sunday afternoon I chose 3 recipes from the cookbook and tripled the recipe and made 9 meals. One I fed to my family and 8 I fed to the freezer. What a joy when my tired body came home from work only to find all I had to do for our evening meal was to pop the casserole into the oven or microwave, make a quick, green salad and shout, "Dinner's ready!"

I continued to feed my freezer with this method until I had over 25 casseroles in reserve.

One day after work my neighbor came by to return a borrowed book and saw my yummy casserole ready to pop into the oven. "Looks good, Carole. What's your recipe?" I began to tell her my story of all the casseroles in my freezer and with delight she asked, "What is the chance of buying one of your casseroles for my dinner tonight?" Much to my surprise I ended up selling her a casserole. Her husband, Carl, loved it and wanted her to repeat the menu. But to his surprise she had to admit it was purchased from her neighbor. "I don't care how you got it," Carl said, "Do it again." With that she told other friends and neighbors how delighted her husband and family were with my instant meals. People began to call asking to buy my freezer out. I have since quit work and now have a home business out of my freezer selling casseroles.

After hearing Carole's story and sharing it with many, Sue and I decided to put together a casserole book for busy women so that you, too, can create tasty, nutritious, and delicious meals to feed to your family.

These kitchen tested recipes will be a thrill and delight to all you share them with.

Joyfully, *Emilie*

How to Use This Book

This casserole book has been designed for busy women! We have divided the 26 casserole recipes into 5 different sets. Each set includes shopping and assembly list. With 5 casseroles in your freezer you will be well stocked with casserole dinners for at least two weeks.

Invite a friend to share in your cooking day for real fun and more efficiency. Plan to double the recipes, take turns providing the kitchen and shopping for ingredients, and split the cost. Another way to fill your freezer is to double or triple your recipes each time you prepare a casserole and freeze the extra. Before you know it your freezer will offer you quite a variety of ready dinners!

Before you begin, familiarize yourself with *Freezing Casseroles*, pp. 7–13. Note in particular that general guidelines are given for thawing and reheating all the casseroles using either microwave or conventional oven. These thawing and reheating times have not been written into each recipe since they will vary considerably for your chosen method and sizes of casseroles.

We have spared you the mystery of unfamiliar ingredients in the *Shopping*, pp. 16–19. We have kept these to a minimum while building higher nutritional quality into the recipes. Nutrient data at the end of each recipe reflects use of particular brands listed in this section or indicated in recipe as preferred.

Every recipe includes per serving exhange values, total calories, protein, fat, carbohydrate, dietary fiber, cholesterol, sodium, and approximate cost. Each menu includes total calories, % of calories in fat, and approximate cost. For help in understanding and using this data, see pp. 72–76.

Finally, In addition to the casseroles we have included 20 bonus recipes plus *Extra Timesaving Tips* (pp. 14–15) to broaden your prepreparations. They will add nutritional value and delicious variety to all your meals.

5

Basic Stock list

See pp. 16-20 for more information on unfamiliar ingredients.

Staples/Seasonings to keep stocked for casseroles:
apple cider vinegar
baking powder
chicken broth
cornstarch or arrowroot powder
garlic (cloves, powder,
   or ready-to-use cut garlic
crystalline fructose
honey
ketsup
lemon juice
olive oil
Sue's "Kitchen Magic" Seasoning
soy sauce
Tabasco sauce
whole wheat pastry flour
   or whole wheat flour
worcestershire sauce

When shopping for these items purchase one or two extra cans or packages, as able:
brown rice
dry beans: pinto, black,
   black-eyed peas
whole grain pastas
almonds, slivered or whole
stoneground cornmeal
tuna, water pack
canned salmon
tomatoes: whole, pieces, sauce
pasta, spaghetti, enchilada sauce
diced green chiles
sliced ripe olives
4 oz. cans mushrooms
pineapple chunks, unsweetened
sliced water chestnuts
Parmesan cheese, canned grated
ground turkey (freezer)
chicken (freezer)
chicken weiners (freezer)
frozen vegetables in 40 oz. bags
   (corn, green beans, peas)
whole grain bread

Spices/Herbs for casserole recipes:
basil
bay leaves
cayenne pepper
chili powder
cumin powder
curry powder
dry mustard
dry parsley flakes
garlic powder
ginger
Italian Seasoning
lemon peel
marjoram
nutmeg
paprika
pepper
rosemary sage
Spike Seasoning
thyme

Keep Available for Chicken Broth Preparation:
fresh carrot, celery, celery leaves, onion, fresh parsley

Stock for Preparing Mixes
whole wheat pastry flour
stoneground cornmeal
buttermilk powder or
   cultured blend
baking powder
baking soda
crystalline fructose
toasted wheat germ (freezer)
Parmesan cheese, grated canned
cinnamon
dill weed
onion powder
raisins
walnuts
frozen blueberries (freezer)
6 oz. frozen orange juice (freezer)
whole grain bread for crumbs

6

Freezing Casseroles

A QUICK OVERVIEW

There are several different ways you can freeze, thaw, and cook casseroles outlined on the following pages. The steps below summarize the general method we prefer to use for convenience as well as for preserving the nutrition and the flavor:

1. Prepare the dish completely, using conventional range top and/or oven for sauteeing, heating, cooking, baking (a few steps may use the microwave.

2. Freeze the casserole in the container in which it will be reheated later.

3. Thaw completely in the microwave on defrost.

4. Reheat in the microwave.

INGREDIENTS

Seasonings:

Both freezing and microwaving can affect the strength of seasonings. Microwaving decreases garlic flavor while freezing increases it. Saltiness increases during microwaving, but decreases in freezing. Pepper can turn bitter and increase in flavor during freezing. Herbs tend to weaken. Here are a few suggestions to overcome the seasoning problem:

1. Measure and add seasonings to thawed casserole just before reheating and serving.

2. Add before freezing, evaluate results after eating the dish and adjust your recipe to taste for future preparation.

3. Combine seasonings when you prepare the casserole, but store them separately in a cupboard. Put them in a tightly covered and labeled container. A small tupperware mini cup would be ideal. Be sure to make a note about adding the seasonings and where they are stored on your frozen casserole label before it is reheated. This will not work, of course with a layered casserole.

Choosing Ingredients:
Ingredients for cassroles that do not freeze well include uncooked raw vegetables, potatoes, hard-cooked eggs, mayonnaise, macaroni, quick-cooking rice.

Preparing Ingredients:
Just barely, or slightly undercook rice, pastas, beans, and vegetables for freezing.

Fat and flour for thickening in saucy dishes can separate during freezing. Thicker sauces separate less. Stir when thawed and again while reheating.

To add frozen vegetables to a casserole for freezing, break up the vegetables, without thawing unless they are cooked before freezing.

Fresh or dried parsley does not have a good appearance after freezing. Add just before reheating or serving. In several dishes, a parsley garnish will really brighten up the casserole!

Bread crumb or cheese toppings become soggy if added to casseroles before freezing. Freeze these in separate packages. Attach to the casserole dish with tape, or make note of other location. Of course, you do not need to freeze these at all, but can add them fresh just before reheating.

Combining Ingredients:
Some casseroles consist of a sauce layered over a starch, such as rice. During freezing the starch absorbs the sauce so that the pleasing saucy texture is diminished. For this reason, you may wish to freeze the rice separately, pouring the sauce over the rice just before heating, or serving each separately at the table. Freezing casserole sauces alone such as *Chicken Curry* or *Turkey-Mushroom Sauce* also allows you to serve them over a variety of choices such as whole grain toast, biscuits, baked or mashed potatoes, whole grain pasta, or brown rice.

Cooked rice may be frozen separately in an airtight ziploc bag. Prepare rice for more than one meal and divide into ziploc bags. To reheat thawed rice in microwave, loosen seal, place bag on plate and cook on full power, about 3 minutes. To reheat on range top, remove rice from bag and steam for 5 minutes. Quick cooking brown rice can be cooked up fresh in 15 to 20 minutes before a meal.

FREEZING METHODS & CONTAINERS

Temperature:
Thoroughly cool casserole before freezing it. Cool in a pan of ice water or in the refrigerator, but not at room temperature, especially dishes with meat in them. Bacteria can multiply in food between 40° and 120° very rapidly.

Foil Method:
Line the baking dish with heavy duty foil before adding casserole, seal tightly, allowing a little headspace for expansion as contents freeze. Label name and date with masking tape and marker pen. Freeze solid, then remove baking dish from the foil package. This allows for more room in the freezer and frees the baking dish for other uses.

It is best not to use foil for tomato dishes or dishes with any high acid content. The acid may react with the foil allowing aluminum residue to get into the food.

Foil may be difficult to remove easily while a dish is still frozen as it can stick to the surface. A light greasing of the inside surface of the foil may help somewhat.

Directly in Dish Method:
Fill dish with casserole allowing at least 1/2 inch headspace for expansion while freezing. To insure airtightness, cover the top of the casserole dish with plastic wrap (suitable for microwaving if you plan to microwave) before securing the lid. You may even wish to cover the entire casserole dish with foil or a sealed plastic bag; it depends on the quality of seal your baking dish may have. Label before freezing with name of dish, date, special cooking/serving reminders.

Containers:
Choose the container that is suitable for the reheating method to be used. To microwave use glass or suitable plastic containers especially designed for both freezer and microwaving. These are widely available in many stores. For conventional oven baking, use any size suitable container that is oven proof up to 400°. Most plasticware designed for microwaving is also listed as oven-safe up to 350-400°; however, our experience suggests it is safer not to use it in a conventional oven!

If planning to freeze casseroles regularly, consider purchasing several casserole dishes just for this purpose so that you can dispense with the foil method which requires extra time and expense. Freezer-to-microwave oven plasticware is especially suitable and quite inexpensive. Choose a good quality that will not chip or crack easily, especially if bumped against a surface while it is freezer cold. Also choose a brand with plastic lids that seal tightly and firmly over the tops of the dishes. *Superseal Microwave Store 'n Serve* brand, for example, excels in durability, effective seals, and has a lifetime guarantee. *Rubbermaid* is also an excellent brand. Difficult-to-remove lids can be eased by running hot water over them first.

To locate these brands, save yourself shopping time by phoning drug stores, variety stores, and department stores in advance. Ask if the sizes you are looking for are in stock as well as the brand. Although these come in a wide variety of sizes and shapes, stock of sizes can vary widely. More durable brands cost a little more but the difference is not significant.

Dishes must be covered airtight to prevent loss of flavor, nutrition, and freezer burn.

Some dishes that can be reheated in a saucepan on top of the stove can be frozen in any container suitable for freezing.

Container Sizes:
Most family recipes fill a 2 to 2 1/2 quart casserole. These recipes usually serve 4 to 6 or more servings. A 1 qt. casserole is enough for 3 adult size servings, or for serving 2 adults and 2 young children. A casserole of 1 1/2 qt. size will serve 4 adults.

Since larger size casserole dishes (2 qt. or larger) require longer to freeze, thaw, and reheat, consider freezing a recipe in two smaller size dishes even if using the entire recipe for one meal. Two smaller casseroles will thaw and reheat more rapidly than one larger one.

Prepare in Quantity:

Small families, singles, and couples will get more than one meal out of most of the recipes. Rather than cut recipes in half, take advantage of the freezer method for efficient quantity preparation. If this is done each time a casserole is prepared, the freezer will quite easily become stocked with several quick meals without setting aside a special casserole making session. If the family uses a full recipe in one meal, consider doubling it and freezing half.

Freezing a large casserole that will last two consecutive evenings is not recommended. Freeze in one container only what you plan to eat in a meal within 24 hours after thawing. Freezing breaks down cell structure of food increasing susceptibility to bacteria growth.

Freeze Quickly:

More flavor and nutrition is retained when a casserole is frozen rapidly. Thoroughly cool before freezing. Do not load over 10% of the freezer space with unfrozen food at any one time. Maintain a freezer temperature of at least 0 degrees F.

Freezer Space:

Most freezers will hold five casseroles at a time. If space is limited take advantage of the 5 casserole assembly plan by freezing three of the casseroles. Refrigerate the remaining two. Use these during the week immediately following preparation.

Length of Time in Freezer:

8 weeks is about the maximum for a frozen casserole to retain its quality. Plan to use it within 3 to 6 weeks. Keep a list of frozen dishes posted in the kitchen and plan them into a written menu.

Relax!

When the casserole assembly session is completed, take a relaxing break with a refreshing drink and plan to go out for dinner.

THAWING METHODS

If the casserole has been frozen in foil, remove it while casserole is still frozen and place in original baking dish.

Refrigerator Method:

Remove dish from freezer the night before serving. Thaw covered. The time required to thaw will depend on the size.

Quick thaw Method:

Quick thawing minimizes nutritional loss. For quickest thawing microwave defrost or reheat from the frozen state in a conventional oven or on range top.

 To Thaw in Microwave

Use the defrost setting on your microwave. The times below are approximate:

1 quart: 35–45 min.   **2 qt: 60–75 min.**
1 1/2 qt: 45–55 min.   **3 qt: 1 hr. + 45–55 min.**

Do not automatically set these times. Test a 1 qt. casserole after 20 minutes, a 1 1/2 qt. after 25 minutes, 2 qt. after 45 minutes, etc., until familiar with how a casserole thaws in your own microwave. Write your own thawing and cooking times on the recipe for future reference.

Loosen the lid or remove the lid, cover firmly with plastic wrap and make a few knife slits in the wrap. Keep dish covered.

 To Thaw in Conventional Oven

Place frozen covered casserole in oven at 350° for approximately 1 1/2 to 3 times longer than you would need for baking in the unfrozen state:

2 quart: Approximately 1 1/2 to 2 hrs.

Room Temperature Method:

This is the least desirable method. Room temperature encourages nutrient lose and bacteria growth.

REHEATING METHODS
Using The Microwave:

For even heating the casserole should be completely defrosted.

Exact cooking or reheating times are not possible. Always test how your casserole is doing before the lowest amount of time suggested below has elapsed. All of the recipes in this book were tested in a 650 Watt Amana Radarange Microwave Oven. Write the times you need to follow in your own recipe book.

 To Reheat in Microwave

Use full or high power setting on your microwave. The times below are approximate:

1 qt: 5–7 min.	2 qt: 7–10 min.
1 1/2 qt: 6–9 min.	3 qt: 9–13 min.

For even heating, stir the dish halfway through the time, if you can, especially if the dish has a sauce thickened with flour. Layered casseroles cannot be stirred easily, but can be given a quarter turn.

If your microwave has a heat probe for automatic temprature control you may wish to reheat the casserole with this method, to an internal temperature of 150°.

 To Reheat in Conventional Oven

The following is the approximate baking time for completely precooked and thawed casseroles. Bake covered at 350°:

Approximately 20 to 30 minutes

To reheat from the frozen state, see *To Thaw in Conventional Oven*, p. 12.

Extra Timesaving Tips

▧ During casserole and meal preparation **have sinkful of soapy water** to receive soiled utensils and dishes. Wash up the collection periodically to keep your work space cleared.

▧ Use the **same pots and fry pans** to cook and saute, wiping or rinsing them out as needed.

▧ Wash and dry **greens for salads** in advance for making quick *Five Minute Salads* (p. 66).

▧ **Prepare mixes** for making quick muffins, cornbread, and biscuits (pp. 67–70).

▧ Purchase and freeze a few **extra packages of whole grain breads:** dinner rolls, buns, French bread, sourdough bread, etc. Take out just what you need for a meal rather than a whole package. Thaw and heat in microwave or conventional oven.

▧ Purchase economy **40 oz. bags of frozen vegetables:** peas, corn, and green beans. Take out only the amount you need for a recipe or side vegetable. Keep bags closed tightly with twist tops.

▧ Purchase, season, brown, and freeze **ground turkey for several meals** at one time; freeze in desired amounts. Wrap packages airtight, first in saran wrap, then foil, or in a special freezer wrap paper. Uncooked frozen meats may be refrozen after they are cooked. It is best not to refreeze this cooked meat in a frozen casserole, however. Use it in dishes not to be frozen.

▧ Freeze **meatloaf and turkey burger patties** using delicious recipes from *Main Dishes.* Wrap packages airtight, first in saran wrap, then foil, or in a special freezer wrap paper. Uncooked frozen meats may be refrozen after they are cooked.

▧ Purchase, precook and freeze several lbs. of **boneless chicken for several meals** at one time; make extra broth and freeze it (pp. 21–22); freeze in desired portions. Use frozen cooked chicken in dishes not to be frozen. Once thawed, frozen meat should not be refrozen.

▧ **Warm items** such as catsup, molasses, honey that are **hard to get out** of the jar **in the microwave.** 40 seconds on full power is about right for 1/4 to 1/2 cup.

Purchase fresh or quick frozen **fish for several meals**. Watch for specials. Rewrap in airtight packages as for freezing chicken (see *note*, p. 21), or in special freezer wrap paper.

Prepare *Ground Turkey Seasoning Mix* (p. 65). Clearly print on the container label: "Use 1/2 tsp. + 1 Tbsp. soy sauce + 2 Tbsp. ketsup per 1 lb." Now you won't need to look up the *Seasoned Ground Turkey* recipe or measure out the spices to prepare it.

Prepare the delicious **crumb coating mixes** for chicken and fish on p. 64. Keep on hand in freezer.

Prepare **soups for the freezer**. Bean, lentil, split pea, and tomato soups freeze especially well. Make and freeze a quantity of *Soup 'n Salad Croutons* (p. 70).

Use a **pressure cooker** to cook dry beans in 1/4 to 1/5 the time. A pressure cooker is an excellent investment. It is also a great time saver for cooking potatoes, fresh green beans, carrots, beets, pot roast, whole chickens. For cooking quantity a pressure cooker beats the microwave! Whatever amount you cook in it, the time is the same. One pressure cooker will last you a lifetime!

Use a **crock-pot** to prepare stews, soups, chicken, or roasts while you are away for the day. Dinner will be done when you return home.

When purchasing **non-perishable items** for one recipe, **buy two and store one** for use another time.

Store ingredients for most convenient access: in front of cuboards, in easiest reach, and nearest the work area where you use them most.

Keep kitchen storage consistent! Organize it to put items back in the same place every time.

Store spices/herbs on turntables. Alphabetize and **number** in this order with bright tape and marker pen. When you purchase a new container of a spice, switch the numbered tape to the new container. A good tape that is easily removed and restickable is Scotch brand flourescent colored plastic tape. A small roll will go a long way. It is a great time saver to locate your spice by alphabet, and replace it by the number!

Shopping

Baking powder Low sodium baking powder, available in health food stores contains no corn, no aluminum, and less sodium than regular baking powder.

Beef broth See **Chicken broth.**

Brown rice is available in all supermarkets. Long grain is closer in texture to white rice than medium or short grain brown rice which are a bit more chewy. Quick Brown Rice (*MJB* in supermarkets, *Arrowhead Mills* in health food stores) is also available. Choose converted white rice (*Uncle Ben's*) over other white rice. It has undergone less nutritional loss.

Butter & Eggs are good wholefoods used in moderation. For explanation see **Eating Right!**, by Emilie Barnes and Sue Gregg, chapts. 18, 20. Our first choice of quality is raw butter produced by Alta Dena Dairy and fertile eggs. Purchase at health food stores or Alta Dena Dairies.

Buttermilk powder for cooking and baking is available in some supermarkets and health food stores. Look in supermarkets for *Saco Cultured Buttermilk Blend.* It is handy for making bread mixes such as muffins, biscuits, and cornbread. If you cannot find it, request the supermarket manager to order it for you, or use fresh buttermilk in place of water in recipes on pp. 67, 69, 70.

Chicken grown without hormones and antibiotics are a safer buy. Inquire about the brands sold in your area. A quality brand produced without hormones sold direct to the consumer and through health food stores is *Shelton Farms*, 204 Loranne, Pomona CA 91767, (714) 623-4361. For more information about chicken, see p. 20.

Chicken broth made while cooking the chicken is our preference (pp. 21–22). If you prefer microwaving chicken, try better brands of chicken broth such as *Hain* and *Health Valley*. Both are available either salted or unsalted, in health food stores and some supermarkets. Less expensive supermarket brands with less salt and no MSG. (monosodium glutamate) include *Swanson Natural Goodness Clear Chicken Broth* and *Pritikin*. Make chicken bouillon cubes your last choice; most contain MSG and are very high in sodium.

Chicken weiners, Health Valley brand, are excellent in flavor, contain no pork, dextrose, sodium nitrate or nitrite and are made from chicken and real food ingredients. Generally only available in health food stores.

Chow mein noodles, though not a high fiber, low fat food, are nice to use occasionally. China Boy brand, made with unbleached white flour and no artificial preservatives, color, or flavors, is available in super-markets in 6 oz. and 12 oz. packages.

Crystalline fructose, fruit sugar, releases less insulin than other sugars in the body. Available in health food stores. Buy a 5 lb. bag for economy. Use half as much as white sugar in most recipes. Looks like white sugar.

Garlic cloves, powder, ready-to-use cut, or crushed can be used interchangeably in all recipes. One clove = 1/8 tsp. powder or 1/2 tsp. ready-to-use cut or crushed.

Ground turkey is available from most supermarkets. Brands vary in the fat content. The amount of skin, light meat, and dark meat used deter-mines the fat content. To obtain ground turkey without skin, you will need to buy whole turkey or turkey parts, skin and bone them, and grind your own. Ground turkey from whole turkey will give you a bargain price but quite a chore in the kitchen. Ground turkey parts will be easier, and the butcher might do it for you, but it will come at a high price. I have settled for a compromise of purchasing ground turkey with the least skin in it available. Turkey Store brand is my current choice. A brand with a lower fat percentage indicates that it contains less skin. Fat percentage by weight is lower than the fat percentage of calories (see comparisons on chart, p. 20). Package labels always list fat percentage by weight which appears more favorable, but confuses the consumer. Shelton Farms markets high quality ground turkey (address under Chicken, p. 16).

Honey for using in casseroles in small amounts is easily purchased at a supermarket. For more generous use and for baking, we recommend using unheated, unfiltered honey from a health food store or a bee keeper. Price ranges vary considerably. Large sizes cost less.

Light sour cream is lower in fat than sour cream. Knudsen Nice n' Light brand contains 40% less fat using cultured grade A pasteurized milk, nonfat milk, cream, kosher gelatin, vegetable enzyme. Look for it in supermarkets. You may find some other brands, as well.

Nuts are more economical in health food stores where they may be purchased in larger quantities than the tiny expensive packages available in supermarkets. Walnuts and unshelled nuts may be an exception.

Oils I recommend olive oil or canola oil, both primarily monounsaturated fat, for cooking. For a summary explanation about these choices see *Main Dishes*, pp. 26-27. Canola oil is readily available in health food stores but may be found in some supermarkets. It is considerably less expensive than olive oil. A little olive oil goes a long way, however. Light olive oils are not so strong in flavor. Don't be too concerned about whether the olive oil is extra virgin, virgin, or pure. It is a very expensive ingredient and you don't need to use very much. Purchase what your budget will allow.

Salt in the form of "unheated" or "sun evaporated only" sea salt is our preference. It contains trace minerals and may be more easily processed by the body. Look for this salt in health food stores. *Orsa Salt* is excellent and may also be ordered directly from American Orsa, Inc., Redmond, Utah 84652.

Spike Seasoning is our favorite all-purpose seasoning containing 39 ingredients. It is, however, about half sea salt. Readily available in health food stores and in some supermarkets.

Soy sauce should be naturally brewed or fermented. *Kikkoman Lite Soy Sauce* contains 200 milligrams sodium per teaspoon. *Kikkoman Milder Soy Sauce* contains slightly less, but the difference is not worth the additional cost. Regular soy sauce contains 314 milligrams sodium per teaspoon. *Kikkoman* contains wheat. If you are allergic to wheat, find a soy sauce made only with soy beans.

Stoneground cornmeal (or ground from whole corn) includes the nutrients of the corn germ. It is generally available only at health food stores.

Stoneground corn tortillas are made from stoneground cornmeal and are generally available only in health food stores. Look for tortillas made only with stoneground cornmeal, lime, and water.

Sue's "Kitchen Magic" Seasoning A wonderful seasoning made from wheat, soy, corn, and alfalfa, this seasoning imparts a salty flavor. It is a hydrolyzed vegetable protein, but contains no MSG (monosodium glutamate). One teaspoon contains 710 milligrams of sodium. When used in recipes, the addition of salt (2,132 mg. sodium per teaspoon) can usually be reduced. To purchase, see order form in back of this book.

Tofu is the most digestible form of soybeans and available in supermarkets in the refrigerated section. It is available in soft, firm, or regular. Health food stores sell tofu made from organically grown soybeans. In any form, tofu is very inexpensive. *Mori Nu* brand comes in a 10.5 oz. size and will keep under refrigeration in the container for several months.

Tomato products such as spaghetti or pasta sauce, enchilada sauce, and ketsup containing nutritionally higher quality ingredients can be found in most health food stores. Look for such brand names as *Westbrae, Johnson's, Health Valley,* and *Hain.* Be sure to read the ingredients labels. For ketsup, *Featherweight* is a brand available in some supermarkets and health food stores.

Tuna Fish Buy water packed only. Many markets now carry 50% reduced salt. A no-salt brand available in some supermarkets or health food stores is *Featherweight* brand.

Whole grain breads of the best nutritional quality are difficult to find in most supermarkets. Health food stores afford the best choices. Look for ingredients labels with all whole grain, no hydrogenated or partially hydrogenated fat, and preferably honey or fruit sugars for sweetenings.

Whole grain pastas are all available. Most are made of wheat in combination with other whole grains or with vegetable powders. Very few supermarkets carry the better whole grain and vegetable pastas. Health food stores generally carry a broad variety. Our first choices are whole wheat or spinach spaghetti and Lasagna noodles, medium flat noodles made of whole amber durum wheat flour or spinach noodles, and macaroni made with enriched durum semolina and soy flour. There is such a wide range of choice, you'll need to experiement to find what you like best, but try to avoid pastas merely prepared with bleached white flour or just "wheat flour."

Whole wheat pastry flour is our first choice for thickening in recipes in place of white flour, although unbleached white flour is preferable to bleached. Whole wheat pastry flour produces lighter quick breads such as muffins, cornbread, and biscuits than whole wheat bread flour, although the latter can be used. Whole wheat pastry flour is generally available only at health food stores. If you own a mill to grind your own pastry grain, grind it fine for use as a thickener for best results.

Worcestershire sauce *Robbie's or Life All Natural* are two brands we recommend, both available at health food stores.

Buying Chicken

What Parts of the Bird?

For convenience I use boneless chicken breast in casseroles most of the time. Compare the cost difference to cooked meat from whole chicken: 1 cup cooked boneless skinned chicken breast prepared from boneless breast with skin @ $3.79 per lb. costs $2.35; 1 cup boneless skinned chicken prepared from whole chicken @ $.99 per lb. costs $1.09. The higher cost of using boneless breast chicken has been used in cost of chicken recipes in this book. The use of whole chicken will net considerable savings on chicken meals!

How Much to Buy

1 lb. of raw boneless chicken will yield 1 5/8 cups skinned boneless cooked chicken. A 3 1/2 lb. whole chicken will yield about 3 1/4 cups skinned boneless cooked chicken.

Buying Ground Turkey

The chart below shows the difference of fat levels between roast turkey, ground turkey, and ground beef. See p. 17 for more information about ground turkey.

3 oz. cooked (85 grams)	Calories	Protein grams	Fat grams	Fat % of Calories	Fat % of Weight
Turkey, light meat, roasted w/out skin [1]	135	25.6	2.75	18%	3%
Turkey, dark meat, roasted w/out skin [1]	164	24.5	6.1	33%	7%
Turkey Store Brand Ground Turkey [2]	174	25	8.7	45%	10%
Louis Rich Brand Ground Turkey [2]	180	21	12	60%	14%
Lean Ground Beef [3]	230	21	16	63%	20%
Regular Ground Beef [3]	245	20	17	66%	21%

[1] **Food Values**, Pennington & Church, Harper & Row, 1985, p. 122.

[2] Package labels.

[3] **Nutrition Wizard**, Michael Jacobson, Center for Science in the Public Interest, 1986

Cooking Chicken or Turkey

There are several ways to cook chicken for casseroles. The methods I use are outlined below.

Preparing the Chicken for Cooking

1. Skin chicken, trim visible fat; wash and pat dry with paper towel, unless planning to stew it.
2. If you want chunks of chicken, cut raw chicken into chunks before cooking. To shred chicken, cook it first, then shred.

To Stew or Crock-Pot

This is the method I use most often. Follow the recipe for **Chicken or Turkey Broth** *(p. 22)* using whatever chicken pieces you want (whole, boneless breast, parts). Use just enough water to cover the chicken unless you want to make a good quantity of broth at the same time. I often add pieces of chicken breast to a pot of brewing broth made with chicken wings or bones. The bits of chicken wing meat and meat scraps from bones usually go into a soup. Chicken breast meat is reserved and frozen for casseroles and salads (see below for freezing).

Cool the chicken enough to handle (30 minutes or less at room temperature, or refrigerate).

To Quick Fry-Simmer

1. Leave chicken pieces whole or cut, as desired, into chunks or strips.
2. Add small amount of oil to hot pan (not needed in a nonstick pan) and immediately add the chicken. Sear on all sides until golden brown. This will seal in the juices.
3. Add about 1/2 cup water, apple cider or wine vinegar. Cover pan tightly, reduce heat to simmer and simmer until the meat is tender, about 20-30 minutes.

To Stir-Fry

Stir fry is quick frying without simmering. Since cooking is short and quick in a hot pan, with or without oil as needed, I use this method only for thin strips of meat that have been marinated. The marinade will tenderize the meat sufficiently so that quick browning is all that is needed to complete the cooking. Meat will be done in 5-10 minutes.

To Steam

This is good for cut poultry parts. Place parts on rack over about an inch of boiling water and cover tightly. Watch the water level so that it doesn't boil away. Steam until tender, about 30 minutes.

To freeze: Divide cooked chicken into portion sizes as desired. Wrap as tightly as possible to exclude air with plastic wrap, then wrap tightly in heavy duty foil. Label with date, amount, and freeze. Use chicken packed dry in this way within one month. Cooked chicken packed in gravy or sauce will keep frozen for up to 6 months.

Chicken or Turkey Broth

This homeprepared chicken broth recipe with salt added contains less than 1/3 the sodium of chicken bouillon cubes and no monosodium glutamate (MSG). It is just 5%-10% the cost of commerically canned brands of broth containing twice or more the amount of sodium. A perfect recipe for the crockpot. I make a large pot and freeze several containers for later use.

AMOUNT: Makes 3 to 4 Quarts
Crock-Pot: Low for 8-10 hours, or High for 3 1/2 to 4 1/2 hours
Range Top: 2-3 hours

1. Snap or crush the bones of chicken or turkey to release juices and gelatinous matter for a richer broth, and to release calcium for more nutrition; place in crock-pot or large pot with remaining ingredients:

   4 to 5 lb. chicken or turkey (wings, backs, and/or bones)
   4 quarts water
   3 tablespoons apple cider vinegar or slice of lemon
   (helps to release calcium from the bones)
   small onion, chopped
   handful celery leaves, chopped
   couple of carrots, chopped
   few sprigs of fresh parsley
   1 bay leaf
   1/2 teaspoon marjoram leaves
   1/4 teaspoon sweet basil leaves
   2 teaspoons salt (optional)

2. Turn crock-pot to low or high, cover and cook or, bring slowly to a boil on range top, cover, lower heat and simmer 2-3 hours adding more water as needed to keep meat or bones covered.

3. Set a colander in a large bowl or pot and pour broth into bowl allowing meat, bones and vegetables collect in the colander.

4. Let cool enough to handle (but not more than 30 minutes); remove vegetables, skin, bone, and store meat as desired.

5. Skim fat off of broth. Refrigerate to allow fat to rise to the top for easier removal, if desired. Strain broth through a double layer of cheese cloth (optional). Freeze in desired portions in freezer containers allowing 1/2" head space. When frozen, run hot water over containers and snap block of broth into heavy duty ziploc freezer bag, or wrap securely in plastic wrap, then tightly with foil.

Per 1 cup with fat removed, based on 4 quart yield (salt included)
   Exchanges: 0.75 Vegetable; 17 Calories, 2 gm. protein (33%), 1 gm. fat (37%), 2 gm. carbohydrate (30%), 276 mg. sodium, $.05 (cost of chicken not included)

VARIATION A highly concentrated stock can be prepared by just covering the bones with water; season as desired, and simmer a full 12 hours, partially covered with lid. Remove fat, strain, and freeze. To use, dilute to desired strength with water. This method takes up less freezer space.

5 Timesaver Casseroles

 **Menus**

Chicken Curry
Brown Rice   (p. 65)
Tossed Salad
w/ Herb Vinegar
Fresh Pineapple
Spears

$1.90
24% Fat
555 Calories

Sausage Strata
Frzn. Green Peas
Carrot-Celery-Pineapple
Salad
w/Sweet Lite Dressing
(Main Dishes, p. 241)
Lemon Ginger Muffins
(Soups & Muffins, p. 73)

$1.35
28% Fat
751 Calories

Favorite Tamalie Pie
Steamed Spinach
Orange & Cucumber Slices
on Greens w/Swt. Mayo.
Dressing *(Main Dishes, p. 241)*
Carrot Sticks
Caraway Rye Bread Bread
(Main Dishes, p. 256)

$1.40
30% Fat
597 Calories

$1.65
22% Fat
842 Calories

$1.40
25 – 28% Fat
765 – 788 Calories

Tuna Fettuchini
One Minute Broccoli (p. 66)
Orange Tossed Salad
w/Sweet Lite Dressing
(Main Dishes, p. 246, 241)
Baked Brown Bread
(Main Dishes, p. 219)

Burrito Fixin's for 2 Burritos:
Best Burrito Beans (3/4 cup)
Mozzarella Cheese, (1/2 cup)
Lettuce, Tomatoes, Onion,
Salsa, Yogurt – Sr. Cream
2 Whole Wheat Tortillas
Radishes, Cucumber,
Carrot Sticks, etc.

Timesaver Shopping list

Meats:
1 to 1 1/2 lbs. boneless
chicken breast
2 lbs. ground turkey

Dairy:
3 eggs
2 cups lowfat milk
1/2 lb. butter
1/2 pint sour or light sour cream
1/2 cup Parmesan Cheese
1/4 lb. cheddar cheese (1 cup)

Grains/Beans/Pasta/Nuts
1/2 lb. brown rice (1 cup)
1 lb. pinto or black beans, dry
8 oz. whole grain noodles*
1/2 lb. stoneground cornmeal*
1/4 cup almonds, slivered or
whole (unroasted, unsalted)
1 slice whole grain bread*

Canned Foods/Misc:
16 oz. tomato, spaghetti,
or pasta sauce
6 1/2 oz. can tuna, water pack
4 oz. can diced green chiles
2 1/4 oz. can sliced ripe olives
24 oz. chicken broth (optional,
see #2 below)

Fresh Produce:
4 small onions
1/2 bunch celery (4 stalks)
1 lb. zucchini
1 small green pepper
1 medium tart green apple

Frozen:
10 oz. frozen corn (2 cups)
1/4 of 10 oz. frozen peas
(1/2 cup)

**Staples/Seasonings/
Spices:**
Check **Basic Stock List**, p. 6
against recipes.

*It may be necessary to purchase these items at a health food store.

Timesaver Assembly

NIGHT BEFORE

1) **Soak beans** for *Burrito Beans* (#1, p. 30).
   If you plan to pressure cook the beans, follow soaking
   instructions at bottom of p. 30.
2) **Cook chicken** for *Curry* in enough water to make 3 cups
   broth for recipe (#2, p. 26).
3) **Set out canned/dry ingredients**, grouping items for each
   recipe together.
4) **Get out freezer containers and cooking pans** (1 large fry
   pan, 1 large pot for *Chili* and cooking pasta, 2 medium
   saucepans for *Brown Rice,* cheese sauce, cornmeal topping).

COOKING DAY

1) **Start** *Brown Rice* for *Curry* (#1, p. 26).
2) **Cook noodles** for *Fettuchini* (#1, p. 29); drain and rinse.
3) **Start cooking beans** for *Burrito Beans* (#2, p. 30), using same pot as for noodles or pressure cook them to reduce cooking time to 30 minutes.
4) **Chop/slice/grate** and place in separate bowls, as needed:
   a) **zucchini**, unpeeled: slice 4 cups, 1/8-1/4" thick (p. 27)
   b) **onions:** chop 3 small, 1 small or medium, 1/4 cup (for all recipes)
   c) **celery:** chop 1 1/2 cups or 6 medium stalks (pp. 26, 29)
   d) **green pepper:** chop 1 small (p. 28)
   e) **almonds** (if whole): chop 1/4 cup (p. 29)
   f) **bread crumbs:** process 1 slice bread in blender to make coarse crumbs (p. 27)
   g) **cheese:** grate 1 cup (p. 27)
   h) **green apple:** wedge, core, and chop one (p. 26)
5) **Saute** zucchini, then ground turkey with onion and seasonings for *Strata* in large fry pan (#1, 2, p. 27); rinse pan for *Tamalie Pie*.
6) Mix 1 lb. ground turkey with seasonings for *Tamalie Pie* (#1, p. 28).

COMPLETE CASSEROLES

1) Complete **Sausage Strata** from #3, p. 27. Do not bake yet. Rinse out saucepan used for cheese sauce to make cornmeal topping for *Tamalie Pie.*
2) **Preheat oven** to 350°.
3) Complete *Tamalie Pie* from #1, p. 28 using same fry pan as for *Strata* and same saucepan as for cheese sauce. **Bake** in oven with *Strata*, 30 minutes for *Strata*, 40-50 minutes for *Tamalie Pie* (or until cornmeal crust is done).
4) Complete **Fettuchini** from #2, p. 29 using same fry pan; place in freezer container and rinse pan for *Curry.*
5) Complete **Curry** from #2, p. 26 using same fry pan.
6) Complete **Burrito Beans** from #3, p. 30.
7) Complete placing casseroles in **freezer containers**, label with names, date, and desired cooking/serving instructions.
8) **Cool** completely in refrigerator; **freeze.**

Chicken Curry

Enjoy the menu, p. 23, one of the three lowest calorie menus in this book!

AMOUNT: 4 to 6 Servings (about 5 to 6 cups sauce, 3 cups rice)

1. Start cooking the **Brown Rice** *(p. 65)*, optional *(see Note below)*

2. Prepare cooked chicken and chicken broth *(pp. 21-22)*:
   1-1 1/2 lb. boneless chicken breast (or 2-3 cups)

3. Saute vegetables and apple in butter or oil until barely tender, about 10 minutes:
   1/4 cup olive oil or melted butter, unsalted
   1 small onion, chopped
   4 medium stalks celery, chopped (about 1 cup)
   1 green tart apple, unpeeled and chopped

4. Mix flour into sauteed ingredients well and stir constantly for about 1 minute; remove from heat and blend in chicken broth:
   1/2 cup whole wheat pastry flour (preferred),
   or 6 tablespoons unbleached white four
   3 cups chicken broth (fat removed)

5. Add and continue to cook and stir until thickened:
   1 tablespoon curry powder, to taste
   1 teaspoon salt (reduce to taste if broth is salted)
   1 teaspoon Spike Seasoning, optional
   1/2 teaspoon paprika
   1/2 teaspoon soy sauce
   1/4 teaspoon garlic powder
   or 1 teaspoon ready-to-use cut garlic

6. Gently stir in the chicken chunks. Pour sauce into separate container or over the rice in baking dish. Cool and freeze. To thaw and reheat see pp. 12-13.

Per serving of 6
(with 1 1/2 lb. boneless chicken and salt in #5; rice and Spike not included, see p. 71):
    Exchanges: 3 Meat, 1.75 Fat, 0.5 Bread, 0.25 Fruit, 0.75 Vegetable
    333 Calories
    35.5 gm. protein (43%), 13.5 gm. fat (36%), 17.5 gm. carbohydrate (21%)
    4 gm. dietary fiber
    87 mg. cholesterol, 268 mg. sodium
    $1.25

Note: We prefer to freeze the sauce and rice separately for this dish, but it may also be frozen together (see *Combining Ingredients*, p. 8). The entire dish will also thaw and reheat more quickly if sauce and rice are frozen in separate containers.

Sausage Strata

Compare the high fat percentage of this recipe (54%) with the menu, p. 23 (28%). This effectively illustrates how the actual percentage of fat consumed in a meal can be altered by the choice of other menu items.

AMOUNT: 6 Servings (approximately 2 qt. casserole)
Oven: 350°   *Bake: 30 minutes, uncovered*

1. Lightly saute zucchini in oil just until crisp-tender and remove from pan:
   2 tablespoons olive oil
   4 cups unpeeled zucchini in 1/8" - 1/4" slices (about 1 lb.)

2. Mix together and brown in the same pan; set aside to cool:
   1 small onion, chopped
   1 lb. ground turkey
   1 teaspoon salt
   1/2 teaspoon nutmeg
   1/2 teaspoon thyme
   1/4 teaspoon sage
   1/16 teaspoon cayenne pepper

3. To make **cheese sauce** blend cornstarch and cold milk together and stir into hot milk. Stir constantly until thickened, about 2 minutes (do not boil). Blend in the cheese:
   1/4 cup cold lowfat milk
   2 tablespoons cornstarch
   1 1/4 cups lowfat milk
   1 cup grated cheddar cheese

4. Combine with cooled turkey and onions:
   3 eggs, beaten with fork
   1 cup whole wheat bread crumbs (1 slice in blender)
   1/8 teaspoon garlic powder

5. Layer cheese sauce, zucchini, turkey mixture in baking dish in 2 layers. Start and end with cheese sauce.

6. Cover and bake at 350° for 30 minutes. Cool and freeze. To thaw and reheat see pp. 12-13.

Per serving of 6
  Exchanges: 3.75 Meat, 0.25 Milk, 1 Fat, 0.25 Bread, 0.75 Vegetable
  336 Calories
  26.5 gm. protein (31%), 21 gm. fat (54%), 13.5 gm. carbohydrate (15%)
  4.5 gm. dietary fiber
  175 mg. cholesterol, 216 mg. sodium
  $.85

Favorite Tamalie Pie

Enjoy the under 600 calorie, economy menu, p. 23, with hot vegetable, salad, and whole grain bread.

AMOUNT: 6 Servings (9" square pan or 2 qt. casserole)
Oven: 350°   **Bake: 40-50 minutes, uncovered**

1. Brown together in large fry pan:
   1 lb. Seasoned Ground Turkey *(p. 65)*
   1 small onion, chopped
   1 small green pepper, chopped
   1/8 teaspoon garlic powder
   or 1/2 teaspoon ready-to-use cut garlic

2. Stir in, simmer briefly, and pour into baking pan:
   2 cups tomato, spaghetti, or pasta sauce
   2 cups frozen corn
   2 1/4 oz. can sliced ripe olives, drained
   1 1/2 teaspoons chili powder
   1/2 teaspoon salt (with tomato sauce only)

3. To make **cornmeal topping**, blend the cornmeal into the cold water. Stir the butter, salt, and cornmeal mixture into the boiling water. Continue stirring over medium-low heat until thickened, about 2 minutes:
   1 cup cold water
   1 cup stoneground cornmeal
   1 cup boiling water
   1 tablespoon butter, unsalted
   1/2 teaspoon salt

4. Spread hot cornmeal mixture evenly over top of pie mixture completely to the edges.

5. Bake uncovered at 350° for 40-50 minutes o until crust is done. Cool and Freeze. To thaw and reheat, see pp. 12-13.

Per Serving of 6
(using tomato sauce and salt in #2)
Exchanges: 2 Meat, 0.75 Fat, 1.75 Bread, 1.5 Vegetable
300 Calories
20.5 gm. protein (25%), 9.5 gm. fat (27%), 39 gm. carbohydrate (48%)
8.5 gm. dietary fiber
49 mg. cholesterol, 508 mg. sodium
$.85

Tuna Fettuchini

Take advantage of the economy, lowfat menu, p. 23.

AMOUNT: 6 Servings (approximately 2 1/2 qt. casserole)

1. To cook pasta, add noodles, salt, and oil to boiling water and cook until barely tender, 5 to 6 minutes; drain and rinse in cold water:
    4 quarts boiling water
    1/4 teaspoon salt
    1 teaspoon oil
    8 oz. whole grain noodles

2. Saute nuts and vegetables in butter:
    1/4 cup melted butter, unsalted
    1/4 cup almonds, slivered or chopped
    1/2 cup celery, chopped
    1/4 cup onion, chopped
    1/4 teaspoon garlic powder
    or 1 teaspoon ready-to-use cut garlic

3. Blend together in large bowl and fold in cooked noodles and sauteed ingredients:
    1 cup sour cream or light sour cream
    1/2 cup Parmesan cheese
    1/2 teaspoon salt

4. Gently fold in:
    6 1/2 oz. can tuna, water pack 50% reduced salt, drained
    1 teaspoon lemon juice (blended into tuna)
    1/2 cup frozen peas (broken apart, but not thawed)

5. Freeze immediately (peas should not be allowed to thaw and other ingredients will already be cool enough).

6. To thaw and reheat, see pp. 12-13.

Per serving of 6 (with sour cream)
    Exchanges: 1.25 Meat, 4.25 Fat, 2 Bread
    406 Calories
    19 gm. protein (18%), 23 gm. fat (50%), 32 gm. carbohydtrate (32%)
    9 gm. dietary fiber
    62 mg. cholesterol, 558 mg. sodium
    $.75

Per serving of 6 (with light sour cream)
    Exchanges: 1.25 Meat, 3.75 Fat, 2 Bread
    384 Calories
    20 gm. protein (21%), 19 gm. fat (45%), 33 gm. carbohydrate (34%)
    9 gm. dietary fiber
    58 mg. cholesterol, 570 mg. sodium
    $.75

Best Burrito Beans

Legumes are especially high in fiber and low in fat. Even with addition of butter or oil for extra flavor, the fat content of this recipe remains low.

AMOUNT: 4 Cups (fits 1 1/2 qt. container best)

1. Soak beans in water overnight or use quick method by bringing beans covered with water to a boil for 3 minutes, and turning off heat for 1 hour before cooking:
   2 cups (1 lb.) uncooked pinto or black beans
   8 cups water

2. Bring undrained beans to a boil, reduce heat and simmer until tender, 2 to 3 hours. Add more water, if needed to prevent burning and sticking to pan. To pressure cook, see **note** below.

3. Saute onion and seasonings in butter or oil:
   1/4 cup melted butter, unsalted, or olive oil
   1 onion, chopped
   1 1/2 tablespoons chili powder
   2 teaspoons cumin powder
   1/4 teaspoon garlic powder
   or 1 teaspoon ready-to-use cut garlic

4. Drain the cooked beans but save the liquid.

5. Combine drained beans with sauteed ingredients. Mash with potato ricer or electric mixer to desired consistency. Add some of the reserved bean liquid, as desired.

6. Mix in:
   1 teaspoon salt, to taste
   4 oz. can diced green chiles, optional

7. Cool and freeze. To thaw and reheat see pp. 12-13.

8. To serve, top with **grated cheddar cheese,** if desired, before reheating beans, or serve with ingredients for making burritos--**grated cheese, shredded lettuce, chopped tomatoes, salsa, whole wheat tortillas, etc.**

Per 1/2 cup (diced chiles included; ingredients in #8 not included)
   Exchanges: 0.5 Meat, 0.5 Fat, 2 Bread, 0.5 Vegetable
   211 Calories
   12.5 gm. protein (25%), 3.5 gm. fat (15%), 31 gm. carbohydrate (60%)
   6.5 gm. dietary fiber
   8 mg. cholesterol (no cholesterol if oil used in step #3), 288 mg. sodium
   $.25

Note: To pressure cook beans, cover **2 cups beans** well with water and add **1/4 cup oil** and **1 tablespoon salt.** Let stand a few hours. Drain, rinse, and cover well with water in cooker, not over one-half full. Process 30 to 35 minutes at 15 lb. pressure.

5 Convenience Casseroles

Menus

Almond Lemon Chicken
Fresh Green Beans (1 cup)
Apple, Carrot, Raisin,
Pineapple Salad
w/Swt. Lite Dressing
(**Main Dishes**, p. 241)
Blueberry Muffins (p. 69)
w/Whipped Butter

$2.10
29% Fat
868 Calories

Salmon Quiche
Tossed Salad
w/Herb Vinegar
Carrot Sticks
Fresh Pineapple

$1.85
38% Fat
600 Calories

Turkey –Mushroom Sauce
Baked Potato in Skin
Frozen or Fresh Green Peas
Sliced Tomatoes & Cucumbers
on Greens
w/Herb Vinegar
Seasonal Fruit Cup

$2.00 –$2.05
14% – 24% Fat
618 – 655 Calories

$2.35
29% Fat
765 Calories

$.80 – $.90
5% – 18% Fat
605 – 706 Calories

Country Creole Peas 'n Corn
Carrot & Celery Sticks,
Cucumber Slices
Minute Bran Muffins
(**Soups & Muffins**, p. 61)
w/Jam

Chicken Spaghetti
Steamed Zucchini Squash
Tossed Salad
w/Thousand Island Dressing
(**Main Dishes**, p. 185)
French Bread
w/Garlic Butter
(**Main Dishes**, p. 261)

Convenience Shopping List

Meats:
3 lbs. boneless chicken breast
1 lb. ground turkey

Dairy:
4 eggs
1 1/2 cups lowfat milk
1/2 lb. butter
1/3 cup Parmesan cheese

Grains/Beans/Pasta/Nuts
1/3 lb. brown rice (2/3 cup)
1 lb. black-eyed peas, dry
8 oz. whole grain spaghetti*
3/4 cup almonds, slivered or whole
  (unroasted, unsalted)

Canned Foods/Misc:
8 oz. can tomato sauce
15 oz. can tomato sauce
2 1 lb. cans stewed tomatoes
2 4 oz. cans mushroom stems &
pieces
15 oz. can salmon (2 cups)
small jar orange marmelade (2 Tbsp.)
48 oz. chicken broth (optional,
  see #2 below)

Fresh Produce:
4 small onions
  (or 3 + 1 green onion)
1 lb. broccoli (3 cups)
2 green peppers

Frozen:
10 oz. frozen corn (or 1 1/2 cups)

Staples/Seasonings/Spices:
Check **Basic Stock List**, p. 6
against recipes.

*It may be necessary to purchase this item at a health food store.

Convenience Assembly

NIGHT BEFORE

1) **Marinate chicken** for *Almond Chicken* (#1, p. 34).
2) **Cook chicken** for *Spaghetti* in enough water to make 1 quart broth for *Almond Chicken* and *Turkey-Mushroom Sauce* (#1, p. 38).
3) **Soak black-eyed peas** for *Creole* (#1, p. 37).
4) **Set out canned/dry ingredients**, grouping items for each recipe together.
5) **Get out freezer containers and cooking pans** (1 large fry pan, 1 large pot for *Creole* and cooking pasta, 2 medium saucepans for cooking *Brown Rice* and broccoli.

COOKING DAY

1) **Cook spaghetti pasta** for *Chicken Spaghetti* (#3, p. 38); drain and rinse; use pot for *Creole.*
2) **Start** *Brown Rice* for *Almond Chicken* (#2, p. 34).
3) Place **black-eyed peas** with water in large pot, season and begin cooking (#2, p. 37).
4) **Chop/slice** and place in separate bowls, as needed:
   a) **onions:** chop 3; chop 2 Tbsp. or 2 Tbsp. green onion (pp. 35, 36, 37, 38)
   b) **green pepper:** chop 2 (pp. 37, 38)
   c) **almonds** (if whole): chop 3/4 cup (pp. 34, 35)
   d) **broccoli:** chop 3 cups flowers and stalks (p. 35)
5) Complete #3, p. 37 for *Creole.*
6) Use *One-Minute Broccoli* recipe on p. 66 to **cook broccoli** for *Quiche* (p. 35); drain and set aside.
7) **Optional:** Preheat oven to 400° and **bake** *Buttermilk Biscuits* for *Turkey-Mushroom Sauce* (#1, p. 36).
8) Prepare **salmon** for *Quiche* (#3, p. 35).
9) Season **ground turkey** for *Turkey-Mushroom Sauce* (#2, p. 36).

COMPLETE CASSEROLES

1) **Make crust** for, and assemble *Quiche* from #1, p. 35.
2) Preheat oven to 375° ; complete *Quiche* from #3, p. 35; **bake.**
3) Complete *Chicken Spaghetti* in large fry pan from #3, p. 38; place in freezer container; rinse and dry pan for *Almond Chicken.*
4) Complete *Almond Chicken* from #3, p. 34 in same pan, using chicken broth reserved from cooking chicken for *Spaghetti,* as needed; place in freezer container; rinse and dry pan for *Turkey-Mushroom Sauce.*
5) Complete *Turkey-Mushroom in Sauce* in same pan from #2, p. 36, using remaining chicken broth reserved from cooking chicken for *Chicken Spaghetti.*
6) Complete *Creole* from #4, p. 37.
7) Complete placing casseroles in **freezer containers,** label with names, date, and desired cooking/serving instructions.
8) **Cool** completely in refrigerator; **freeze.**

Almond Lemon Chicken

With green beans, salad, and whole grain muffins, we've put this 47% fat recipe in a 29% fat menu, p. 31!

AMOUNT: 6 Servings (9 x 13" pan or 1 1/2 qt. casserole)

1. Slice each chicken piece in 3 or 4 lengthwise strips and marinate in marinade of remaining ingredients 2 hours or longer:
   1 1/2 lb. boneless chicken breast (skinned, fat trimmed)
   5 tablespoons lemon juice
   3 tablespoons prepared mustard, no salt added *(see Note below)*
   2 tablespoons olive oil
   1/4 teaspoon garlic powder
   1/4 teaspoon pepper

2. Start cooking **Brown Rice** *(p. 65)*.

3. Saute nuts in butter until golden in fry pan and remove from pan:
   2 tablespoons melted butter, unsalted
   1/2 cup almonds, slivered or chopped

4. Drain chicken, saving marinade, and brown on both sides in same fry pan, 6 to 10 minutes; blend in and cook liquid down to about 2/3 the volume:
   reserved marinade
   2 cups Chicken Broth *(p. 22)*, fat removed
   blend of 2 tablespoons each cold water and cornstarch

5. Stir in:
   sauteed almonds
   2 tablespoons orange marmelade
   1/4 teaspoon cayenne pepper

6. Layer chicken strips diagonally over cooked rice in baking dish and pour sauce evenly over all.

7. Cool and freeze. To thaw and reheat see pp. 12-13.

Per serving of 6
  Exchanges: 3 Meat, 3 Fat, 0.5 Bread, 0.25 Vegetable
  359 Calories
  36 gm. protein (40%), 18.5 gm. fat (47%), 11.5 gm. carbohydrate (13%)
  2 gm. dieatry fiber
  98 mg. cholesterol, 170 mg. sodium
  $1.30

Note: Look for *Featherweight* brand products, such as prepared mustard, both in supermarkets and healthfood stores. This brand specializes in no-salt items.

Salmon Quiche

The fatty acids of salmon are considered especially beneficial to health. For variation, use 1/4 cup oil in place of butter in the crust (#1 below).

AMOUNT: 6 Servings (9" or 10" pie plate)
Oven: 375°   *Bake: 30–40 minutes*

1. To make **crust,** blend flour and salt; cut in the butter with pastry blender or 2 table knives until dough is size of small peas. Lightly stir water in with fork, but do not overwork dough:
   1 1/2 cups whole wheat flour
   1/2 teaspoon salt
   1/3 cup soft butter, unsalted
   1/4 cup ice cold water

2. Place dough (it will look crumbly) into a buttered glass pie plate. Shape dough into pie plate with fingers, shaping onto sides, then the bottom. Flute edges.

3. Arrange over bottom of crust:
   3 cups cooked broccoli *(p. 66)*, **using small flowers and chopped stalks**
   1/4 cup slivered or chopped almonds
   2 tablespoons chopped yellow or green onion
   15–16 oz. can (2 cups) salmon, drained (crumble between fingers, including soft bones, an excellent calcium source)

4. Blend together and pour evenly over all:
   4 eggs, slightly beaten
   1 1/2 cups lowfat milk
   1/3 cup Parmesan cheese
   1/2 teaspoon salt
   1/4 teaspoon cayenne pepper, to taste
   1/8 teaspoon nutmeg
   paprika garnish

5. Bake 30 to 40 minutes at 375° until knife comes clean out of the center.

6. Cool and freeze. To thaw and reheat see pp. 12–13.

Per serving of 6
    Exchanges: 3 Meat, 0.25 Milk, 2.75 Fat, 1.75 Bread, 1 Vegetable
    474 Calories
    29 gm. protein (23%), 25.5 gm. fat (46%), 38 gm. carbohydrate (31%)
    7 gm. dietary fiber
    207 mg. cholesterol, 919 mg. sodium
    $1.25

Turkey-Mushroom Sauce

For a saucier consistency freeze sauce alone . Serve over baked potatoes, whole grain toast, brown rice, or whole wheat biscuits. May be frozen over top of biscuits, if desired. When frozen together, the biscuits will soak up most of the sauce.

AMOUNT: 4 Cups Sauce (1 1/2 qt container for sauce only)
5 Cups Sauce with yogurt/sour cream added
12 Biscuits (9 x 13" baking dish with biscuits)

1. Bake a recipe of **Buttermilk Biscuits**, optional *(p. 70)*.

2. Mix together and brown in fry pan:
   1 lb. *Seasoned Ground Turkey* *(p. 65)*
   1 small onion, chopped
   4 oz. can mushroom stems & pieces, drained

3. Blend chicken broth, flour, and seasonings together well with a wire whisk and stir into browned turkey; stir and cook until thickened:
   2 cups *Chicken Broth* *(p. 22)*, not warmed; fat removed
   3/4 cup whole wheat pastry flour (preferred)
   or 6 tablespoons unbleached white flour
   1 teaspoon garlic powder
   2 tablespoons *Sue's "Kitchen Magic" Seasoning* *(p. 18)*

4. Pour sauce over biscuits (optional).

5. Cool and freeze. To thaw, see p. 12.

6. To thawed sauce add before reheating (optional):
   1 cup sour cream or lowfat yogurt (or 1/2 of each)
   (or 1 cup light sour cream)
   2 teaspoons dry or 1/4 cup fresh minced parsley

7. To reheat, see p. 13 (do not allow sour cream or yogurt to boil).

Per 1 cup serving (biscuits, sour cream, yogurt excluded)
  Exchanges: 3 Meat, 1.5 Bread, 1 Vegetable
  308 Calories
  28.5 gm. protein (35%), 9.5 gm. fat (26%), 31.5 gm. carbohydrate (39%)
  5 gm. dietary fiber
  66 mg. cholesterol, 1430 mg. sodium, $1.05

Per 1 cup serving of sauce only with sour cream (half sour cream/half lowfat yogurt)
  Exchanges: 2.25 Meat, 2.25 (1.125) Fat, (1.125) Milk, 1.125 Bread, 0.75 Vegetable
  345 (310) Calories
  24 (25) gm. protein (27-31%), 27.5 gm. carbohydrate (34%) 17 (12.5) gm. fat (35-43%)
  4 gm. dietary fiber
  73 (64) mg. cholesterol, 1169 (1172) mg. sodium, $1.00 ($.95)

VARIATIONS: Use **1 cup sliced fresh mushrooms** in place of canned. Use **1/2 lb. ground turkey** and **2 cups fresh or two 4 oz. cans mushrooms** for lower calories and fat.

Country Creole Peas 'n Corn

Our Country Creole menu (p. 31) shares first place with the Barley Casserole menu (p. 39) for lowest cost and percentage of fat. Great vegetarian dishes!

AMOUNT: 6 to 8 Servings (8-9 cups or 2 1/2 qt. casserole)

1. Soak peas in water 1 to 3 hours or overnight:
   2 cups (1 lb.) uncooked black-eyed peas
   8 cups water
2. Bring peas in water to a boil, add seasonings and boil 3 minutes; reduce heat to simmer:
   1 bay leaf
   1 teaspoon Italian Seasoning
   1/2 teaspoon rosemary
3. Saute vegetables in butter (optional for best flavor) or add unsauteed vegetables directly to the peas as they cook:
   2 tablespoons butter, melted
   1 onion, chopped
   1 green pepper, chopped
4. Continue to cook until peas are almost tender, about 1 1/2 hours. Add more water, if needed.
5. Add remaining ingredients, stirring in the corn after casserole cools completely, just before freezing:
   1 lb. can stewed tomatoes
   8 oz. can tomato sauce
   1/2 stick (1/4 cup) butter (optional for added flavor)
   2 tablespoons honey
   1/2 teaspoon salt
   1 1/2 cups frozen corn
6. To reheat, turn frozen casserole out into a saucepan over direct low heat. Add a couple cups of water. When heat has thawed the dish completely, bring to a boil, lower to simmering and simmer 30 minutes. Add more water as needed. Recipe should be quite soupy. Remove bay leaf before serving.

Per serving of 6 (butter excluded)
Exchanges: 0.75 Meat, 3 Bread, 2 Vegetable
302 Calories
16 gm. protein (21%), 1 gm. fat (3%), 60 gm. carbohydrate (76%)
12 gm. dietary fiber
312 mg. sodium, $.45

Per serving of 6 (using unsalted butter)
Exchanges: 0.75 Meat, 2.25 Fat, 3 Bread, 2 Vegetable
403 Calories
16.5 gm. protein (16%), 12.5 gm. fat (27%), 60 gm. carbohydrate (57%)
12 gm. dietary fiber
31 mg. cholesterol, 314 mg. sodium, $.55

Chicken Spaghetti

A lowfat dish refreshingly different from spaghetti with hamburger.

AMOUNT: 6 to 8 Servings (2 qt. to 2 1/2 qt. casserole)

1. Prepare cooked chicken and chicken broth *(pp. 21–22):*
   1 1/2 lb. boneless chicken breast (skinned, fat trimmed)

2. Save extra chicken broth for *Almond Lemon Chicken, (p. 34)* and for *Turkey-Mushroom Sauce (p. 36)* or, refrigerate or freeze for another use.

3. To cook pasta, add spaghetti, salt, and oil to boiling water and cook just until barely tender, 7 to 10 minutes; drain and rinse in cold water:
   4 quarts boiling water
   1/4 teaspoon salt
   1 teaspoon oil
   8 oz. package whole grain spaghetti

4. Saute vegetables in oil or butter until barely tender in large pan:
   2 tablespoons olive oil or unsalted butter, melted
   1 small onion, chopped
   1 green pepper, cut in small pieces (optional)
   4 oz. can mushroom stems & pieces (optional)

5. Stir in and cook over low heat for 5 minutes:
   15 oz. can tomato sauce (about 2 cups)
   1 lb. can stewed tomatoes
   1 teaspoon Italian Seasoning
   1/2 teaspoon salt

6. Add chicken, stirring carefully so chicken pieces do not break up; cook 5–10 minutes longer.

7. Layer chicken and sauce on top of spaghetti in casserole dish.

8. Cool and freeze. To thaw and reheat see pp. 12–13.

Per serving of 6 (using olive oil)
   Exchanges: 2.75 Meat, 1 Fat, 2 Bread, 2.5 Vegetable
   413 Calories
   40 gm. protein (40%), 8.5 gm. fat (19%), 42 gm. carbohydrate (41%)
   3.5 gm. dietary fiber
   87 mg. cholesterol, 540 mg. sodium
   $1.55

VARIATIONS: Use **1 lb. *Seasoned Ground Turkey*** *(p. 65)* in place of chicken. For vegetarian spaghetti omit meat altogether. It is quite delicious with a sprinkling of Parmesan cheese.

5 Quick Casseroles

Menus

Barley Casserole
One Minute Broccoli (p. 66)
Three Bean Salad
on Greens
w/Marvelous Marinade
(**Main Dishes**, p. 243)
Apple Raisin Muffins (p. 69)
w/Whipped Butter

$.95
12% Fat
706 Calories

Chicken Pot Pie
Cole Slaw
w/Swt. Lite Dressing
(**Main Dishes**, p. 241)
Seasonal Fruit Cup

$1.70
27% Fat
617 Calories

Casserole a la Tuna
Leafy Green Salad
w/ Soup 'n Salad
Croutons (p. 70)
w/Sue's House Dressing
(**Main Dishes**, p. 238)
Buttermilk Biscuits (p. 70)
w/Jam

$1.35
28% Fat
843 Calories

$1.75
26% Fat
625 Calories

$1.20
27% Fat
624 Calories

Emilie's Noodle Bake
Tossed Salad
w/Herb Vinegar
French Bread
w/Garlic Butter
(**Main Dishes**, p. 261)

Sweet 'n Sour Beans
Carrot & Celery Sticks
w/Cherry Tomatoes
Cornbread (p. 67)
w/Whipped Butter

Quick Shopping List

Meats:
4-5 lbs. chicken wings
   or 1 1/2 lb. boneless
   chicken breast
2 lbs. ground turkey

Dairy:
1 egg
1 1/2 cups nonfat milk
1/4 lb. butter
1 pint lowfat cottage cheese

Grains/Beans/Pasta/Nuts
1/2 lb. brown rice (or 1 cup)
1/2 lb. pearled barley (or 3/4 cup)
8 oz. spinach noodles*
1/2 lb. stoneground cornmeal*
   (or 3/4 cup)
1/2 cup almonds, slivered, sliced or
   whole (unroasted, unsalted)

Staples/Seasonings/Spices:
Check **Basic Stock List**, p. 6
against recipes.

Canned Foods/Misc:
16 oz. spaghetti, or pasta sauce (2 cups)
6 1/2 oz. can tuna, water pack
8 3/4 oz. can garbanzo beans (optional)
2 15 oz. cans butter beans
2 17 oz. cans green lima beans
2 15 1/4 oz. cans red kidney beans
2 1 lb. cans Heinz Vegetarian Beans in
   Tomato Sauce or baked beans if
   not available
8 oz. can sliced water chestnuts
1 2-4 oz. can mushroom stems & pieces
   (unless fresh are purchased)
small jar molasses (or 1/4 cup)
40 oz. chicken broth; 16 oz. may be beef
   (optional, see #1 below)

Fresh Produce:
5 medium onions
1 bunch celery (8 stalks)
2 medium carrots
2 green peppers
1 cup mushrooms (about 3 oz,), unless
   canned mushrooms are used

Frozen:
10 oz. frozen green peas (2 cups)

*It may be necessary to purchase these items at a health food
   store.

Quick Assembly

NIGHT BEFORE

1) **Cook chicken** and **broth** for *Pot Pie* and, if desired, for
   Barley Casserole and *Casserole a la Tuna*, (#1, 2, p. 43).
2) Use recipe on p. 65 to **season ground turkey** for *Noodle
   Bake* (#2, p. 45); **brown** it and refrigerate.
3) **Season, brown,** and **refrigerate ground turkey** for
   Sweet 'n Sour Beans (#1, p. 46).
4) **Set out canned/dry ingredients,** grouping items for each
   recipe together.
5) **Get out freezer containers and cooking pans** (1 large fry
   pan, 1 large pot for cooking pasta, 1 medium saucepan for
   rice, 1 medium mixing bowl for *Pot Pie* crust and *Noodle
   Bake*, and 1 large mixing bowl for *Sweet 'n Sour Beans*).

COOKING DAY

1) Start **Brown Rice** for *Casserole a la Tuna* (#1, p. 44).
2) **Cook noodles** in large pot for *Noodle Bake* (#1, p. 45); drain and rinse.
3) **Brown barley** in large fry pan for *Barley Casserole* (#1, p. 42); place in casserole freezer dish for baking; wipe out pan to use for *Pot Pie.*
4) **Chop/slice** and place in separate bowls, as needed:
   a) **onions**, medium: chop 2, slice 2 (pp. 42, 43, 44, 46)
   b) **green pepper:** chop 2 small (pp. 42, 44)
   c) **mushrooms:** slice 1 cup if canned ones not used (p. 42)
   d) **carrots:** slice or coarsely chop 2 (p. 43)
   e) **celery:** chop 4 stalks, slice 4 stalks on diagonal (pp. 43, 44)
   f) **almonds** (if whole): chop 1/2 cup (p. 44)

COMPLETE CASSEROLES

1) **Preheat oven** to 350°; complete **Barley Casserole** for baking (#1, 2, p. 42); **bake.**
2) In large fry pan complete *Pot Pie* except for crust topping (#3, 4, p. 43); place in freezer container and rinse out pan for *Casserole a la Tuna.*
3) Complete **Pot Pie** from #5, p. 43 mixing crust topping in medium mixing bowl; rinse bowl for assembling *Noodle Bake;* **Bake Pot Pie** in oven with *Barley Casserole.*
4) Complete **Casserole a la Tuna** using large fry pan; place in freezer container; rinse fry pan for *Sweet 'n Sour Beans.*
5) Combine **Noodle Bake** ingredients (#2, p. 45) in mixing bowl; place in freezer container.
6) Complete **Sweet 'n Sour Beans** from #2, p. 46 in large fry pan and large mixing bowl; rinse out pan to saute remaining vegetables for *Barley Casserole.*
7) **Saute vegetables** for *Barley Casserole* (#3, p. 42); set aside.
8) Complete placing casseroles in **freezer containers,** label with names, date, and desired cooking/serving instructions.
9) **Cool** completely in refrigerator. **Add sauteed vegetables** set aside to **Barley Casserole** (#4, p. 42). **Freeze casseroles.**

Barley Casserole

A hearty dish that is truly vegetarian when water is substituted for broth. A great economy meal and only 12% fat (p. 39)!

AMOUNT: 6 Servings (6 1/2 cups or 2 qt. casserole)
Oven: 350°   *Bake: 1 1/2 - 2 hours, covered*

1. Brown the barley in a dry fry pan over medium heat for about 10 minutes, stirring frequently and combine with remaining ingredients in casserole baking dish:
   3/4 cup pearl barley, uncooked
   2 cups boiling hot *Chicken Broth* *(p. 22)* **or beef broth** (or water with ***Sue's "Kitchen Magic"***)
   2 teaspoons soy sauce
   1 1/2 teaspoons *Sue's "Kitchen Magic" Seasoning* *(p. 18)* **or 1/2 teaspoon salt if seasoning not available**
   8 1/2 or 8 3/4 oz. can garbanzo beans, 50% salt reduced (optional), **drained, rinsed** *(see Note, p. 46)*
   2 oz. or 4 oz. can mushroom stems & pieces (or fresh mushrooms--see #4 below)
   1/2 to one 8 oz. can sliced water chestnuts, drained

2. Cover and bake at 350° for 1 1/2 to 2 hours until barley is tender and liquid is absorbed.

3. While casserole bakes saute vegetables in oil just until lightly cooked (green pepper should keep bright color):
   2 tablespoons olive oil
   1/2 onion, chopped
   1 small green pepper, chopped
   1 cup fresh mushrooms, sliced (if canned mushrooms are not used)

4. Cool baked casserole and fold in the sauteed vegetables just before freezing. To thaw and reheat see pp. 12-13.

Per serving of 6
(with garbanzo beans, and fresh mushrooms)
   Exchanges: 0.5 Meat, 1 Fat, 1.5 Bread, 1 Vegetable
   198 Calories
   6 gm. protein (11%), 6 gm. fat (26%), 33 gm. carbohydrate (63%)
   5 gm. dietary fiber
   426 mg. sodium
   $.35

Chicken Pot Pie

This is a great recipe for chicken wings, backs, etc.!

AMOUNT: 6 to 8 Servings (2 qt. to 2 1/2 qt. casserole)

Oven: 350º   **Bake: 30-40 minutes, uncovered**

1. Prepare chicken and broth *(pp. 21-22)*; skin, bone, cut into pieces as needed:

   4-5 lbs. chicken wings or 1 1/2 lb. boneless (about 3 cups)

2. Reserve extra broth for *Barley Casserole* and *Casserole a la Tuna*, if desired *(pp. 42, 44)*.

3. Saute vegetables in butter or water about 7 minutes, then add the chicken broth and seasonings and bring to boil; remove from heat:

   1/2 stick (1/4 cup) butter, melted (optional for added flavor)
   1/2 large or 1 medium onion, chopped
   4 stalks celery, chopped
   2 medium carrots, sliced or coarsely chopped
   1 1/2 cups chicken broth (fat removed)
   3/4 teaspoon salt
   1/4 teaspoon pepper
   1/4 teaspoon thyme

4. Blend flour into milk, stir into broth mixture, return to heat and cook, stirring until thickened. Add peas and chicken:

   1 cup cold nonfat milk
   1/4 cup whole wheat pastry flour (or unbleached white flour)
   cooked chicken
   10 oz. package (2 cups) frozen peas

5. To make **crust** blend dry ingredients, cut in butter until crumbly; combine and stir in liquids just until moistened:

   3/4 cup stoneground cornmeal
   3/4 cup whole wheat or whole wheat pastry flour
   1 1/2 teaspoons crystalline fructose or sugar
   1 1/2 teaspoons baking powder *(low sodium preferred, p. 16)*
   3/4 teaspoon salt
   3 tablespoons soft unsalted butter
   1 large egg, beaten
   1/2 cup nonfat milk

6. In casserole dish spread evenly over sauce. Bake at 350º for 30-45 minutes or until crust is done.

7. Cool and freeze. To thaw and reheat see pp. 12-13.

Per serving of 6
(with low sodium baking powder; butter for sauteeing in #2 excluded, see p. 71)
Exchanges: 3 Meat, 0.25 Milk, 1.125 Fat, 2.5 Bread, 1 Vegetable
465 Calories, 43.5 gm. protein (37%), 12 gm. fat (23%), 47.5 gm. carbohydrate (40%)
10.5 gm. dietary fiber, 139 mg. cholesterol, 808 mg. sodium, $1.35

Casserole a la Tuna

Serve with salad and biscuits for an easy economy meal, p. 39.

AMOUNT: 4 to 5 Servings (Approximately 2 qt. casserole)

1. Make **Brown Rice** *(p. 65)*.

2. Saute green pepper in a little water or oil (optional for flavor) about 2 minutes, remove it and add remaining ingredients to pan to saute about 7 minutes:
   1/2 green pepper, cut in thin strips
   1 onion, chopped (about 1 cup)
   4 stalks celery, sliced thinly on diagonal (about 1 cup)
   1/2 cup almonds, slivered, sliced, or chopped

3. Stir in and cook and stir about 7 minutes to absorb some of the liquid:
   1 cup Chicken Broth *(p. 22)*
   3 cups cooked brown rice
   1 teaspoon Spike Seasoning (optional, but good)
   1/2 teaspoon salt
   1/4 teaspoon garlic powder
   or 1 teaspoon ready-to-use cut garlic

4. Add:
   6 1/2 oz. can tuna, water pack 50% salt reduced, drained
   1/2 to one 8 oz. can water chestnuts, sliced, drained (optional)
   sauteed green pepper

5. Place in casserole dish, cool and freeze. To thaw and reheat see pp. 12-13.

Per serving of 4
(with 1/2 can water chestnuts; oil for sauteeing, Spike Seasoning not included, see p. 71)
    Exchanges: 1 Meat, 2.25 Fat, 2.25 Bread, 1.75 Vegetable
    361 Calories
    19 gm. protein (21%), 11 gm. fat (27%), 49 gm. carbohydrate (52%)
    10 gm. dietary fiber
    49 mg. cholesterol, 1,053 mg. sodium
    $.80

Extra Timesaver Tip: Keep your utility knives well sharpened! Use a sharpening steel or sharpening stone for easy and fast sharpening. It's amazing how much easier sharp knives make the vegetable cutting job!

Emilie's Noodle Bake

A really simple casserole to make! Make a very quick meal with tossed salad and French bread . Only 26% fat (p. 39)!

AMOUNT: 6 Servings (2 1/2 qt. casserole)

1. To cook pasta, add noodles, salt, and oil to boiling water and cook just until barely tender, 7 to 10 minutes; drain and rinse in cold water:
   4 quarts boiling water
   1/4 teaspoon salt
   1 teaspoon oil
   8 oz. package spinach noodles

2. Brown the turkey and combine with remaining ingredients:
   1 lb. *Seasoned Ground Turkey* *(p. 65)*
   2 cups pasta or spaghetti sauce
   1 pint (2 cups) lowfat cottage cheese
   cooked noodles

3. Place in casserole, cool and freeze. To thaw and reheat see pp. 12–13.

Per serving of 6
Exchanges: 3 Meat, 0.25 Fat, 1.75 Bread, 2 Vegetable
364 Calories
32.5 gm. protein (36%), 9.5 gm. fat (24%), 37 gm. carbohydrate (40%)
8 gm. dietary fiber
50 mg. cholesterol, 738 mg. sodium
$1.00

Extra Timesaver Tip: Frozen casseroles and preprepared home mixes are not the only way to save last minute time! Establish the habit of putting together any main dish recipe the evening or morning before serving. Refrigerate it until time to bake or cook it for the evening meal. For baked items, measure out dry ingredients and liquid ingredients, storing separately until time to bake. Or measure out the water and grain for making rice, the water for boiling pasta, etc. Do all time-consuming jobs possible ahead of time. Have salad dressings (commercial or homeprepared) readily available to last at least for the week.

With these things done, the evening meal can be whipped together in minutes with just an oven to turn on, a vegetable to heat, a salad to assemble. Have the table set in advance, in a spare minute or two (a good job for children). Preparation under pre-dinner time pressure is more tiring than advanced preparation under more relaxed conditions!

Sweet 'n Sour Beans

Absolutely yummy, easy to prepare, and takes freezing especially well! So low in fat that you can enjoy butter on the bread while keeping the fat level low (see menu, p. 39).

AMOUNT: Easily 12 Servings (12 to 13 cups; divide as desired)

1. Blend turkey with seasonings and brown; remove from pan:
   1 lb. ground turkey
   1 teaspoon salt
   1/2 teaspoon nutmeg
   1/2 teaspoon sage
   1/2 teaspoon thyme
   1/16 teaspoon cayenne pepper

2. Add onions to the pan with a little water and cook covered until tender, but not browned; drain off excess water, add remaining ingredients and simmer covered for 20 minutes:
   2 medium onions, sliced and separated into rings
   1/3 cup apple cider vinegar
   1/4 cup honey
   1 teaspoon prepared mustard, no salt added *(see Note, p. 34)*
   1 teaspoon salt
   1/2 teaspoon garlic powder

3. In large bowl combine onion mixture and turkey with beans:
   2　15 oz. cans butter beans, drained and rinsed *(Note below)*
   2　17 oz. cans green lima beans, drained and rinsed
   2　15 1/4 oz. cans red kidney beans, drained and rinsed
   2　1 lb. cans Vegetarian Beans in Tomato Sauce (Heinz, available in supermarkets; if not available, use baked beans)

4. Check the taste. If desired, blend together and stir in:
   1/4 cup molasses
   1/4 cup ketsup, no salt added *(p. 19)*
   1 teaspoon worcestershire sauce

5. Cool and freeze. To thaw and reheat, see pp. 12–13.

Per 1 cup serving
  Exchanges: 1.75 Meat, 2.5 Bread, 0.5 Vegetable
  299 Calories
  18 gm. protein (24%), 3 gm. fat (10%), 49.5 gm. carbohydrate (66%)
  10.5 gm. dietary fiber
  22 mg.
  cholesterol, 1118 mg. sodium (see Note below)
  $.75

Note: The high sodium content of canned beans may be reduced by 40% by rinsing drained beans thoroughly with running water of 1 minute.

Chicken Hawaiian
Brown Rice (p. 65)
Chinese Spinach Salad
w/Sue's House Dressing
(Main Dishes, p. 244, 238)
Buttermilk Biscuits (p. 70)
w/Whipped Butter

$1.90
29% Fat
814 Calories

Little Saucy Meat Balls
Mashed Potatoes
Fresh or Frozen Green Beans
Carrot–Raisin Salad
w/Swt. Lite Dressing
(Main Dishes, p. 241)

$1.25
26% Fat
536 Calories

Autumn Stew
Grated Carrot Salad w/Pineapple
w/Swt. Mayonnaise Dressing
(Main Dishes, p. 241)
Pumpernickel Bread
(Main Dishes, p. 258)
w/Jam

$1.20
24% Fat
470 Calories

$1.50
28% Fat
725 Calories

$1.55
29% – 33% Fat
771 – 798 Calories

Noodle Parmesan Supreme
Rainbow Salad (Sliced
Tomatoes & Cucumbers, centered
with Grated Carrots on Greens)
w/Herb Vinegar
Blueberry Muffins (p. 69)
w/Jam
Watermelon Wedges

Chili Gourmet
Parmesan Greens
w/Thousand Island Dressing
(Main Dishes, p. 246, 185)
Carrot Sticks
Pineapple Corn Muffins (p. 67)
w/Honey

Make•Ahead Shopping List

Meats:
1 lb. boneless chicken breast
2 lbs. ground turkey

Dairy:
1/4 cup nonfat milk
1/8 lb. butter
1 cup sour or light sour cream
1/2 cup Parmesan cheese

Grains/Beans/Pasta/Nuts
1/2–1 lb. brown rice (optional)
8 oz. whole grain noodles*
1/4 cup almonds, slivered, or whole
    (unroasted, unsalted)
1/2 cup roasted cashews (unsalted)*
1 slice whole grain bread*

Staples/Seasonings/Spices:
Check **Basic Stock List**, p. 6
against recipes.

Canned Foods/Misc:
2 1 lb. cans tomato pieces
29 oz. can whole tomatoes
15 oz. can kidney beans
27 oz. can kidney beans
20 oz. can pineapple chunks,
    unsweetened
2 oz. jar pimiento
12 to 19 oz. box tofu, firm or regular

Fresh Produce:
3 onions
1/2 bunch celery (or 2 cups)
2 green peppers
1/2 bunch parsley
1 lb. yellow squash (as banana)
1 lb. summer squash (as patty pan,
    scallop or yellow crockneck)
2 medium zucchini
1 lb. broccoli (1 cup flowers)
1 small eggplant
1 lb. mushrooms

Frozen:
1/4 of 10 oz. frozen peas (1/2 cup)

*It may be necessary to purchase these items at a health food store.

Make•Ahead Assembly

NIGHT BEFORE

1) **Cook** and **refrigerate chicken** for *Chicken Hawaiian* (#1, p. 50).
2) **Freeze tofu** for *Chili* (#1, p. 54).
3) **Season, brown,** and **refrigerate ground turkey** for *Autumn Stew* (#1, p. 52).
4) **Set out canned/dry ingredients,** grouping items for each recipe together.
5) **Get out freezer containers and cooking pans** (1 large fry pan, 1 large pot for cooking pasta, *Chili, Autumn Stew*, saucepan for rice (optional).

COOKING DAY

1) **Optional: Start** *Brown Rice* for *Chicken Hawaiian* and/or *Meatballs* (pp. 50, 51), if desired.
2) **Chop/slice** and place in separate bowls as needed:
   a) **onions:** chop 2, chop 1/3 cup (pp. 50, 51, 54)
   b) **celery:** slice 2 cups on diagonal (p. 50)
   c) **yellow squash:** 1 lb. peeled, cut in 2" pieces (p. 52)
   d) **summer squash:** 1 lb. cut in 2" pieces (p. 52)
   e) **zucchini,** unpeeled: 1 medium, sliced (p. 52), 1 small, chopped (p. 53)
   f) **mushrooms:** 1/2 lb. quartered (p. 46), 2 cups sliced (p. 54)
   g) **small eggplant:** peeled, cut in 2" pieces (p. 52)
   h) **green pepper:** 1 cut in medium pieces (p. 52) 1 chopped (p. 54)
   i) **broccoli:** 1 cup flowers (p. 53)
   j) **almonds** (if whole): chop 1/4 cup (p. 53)
3) **Cook noodles** and **vegetables** for *Noodle Parmesan* (#1, p. 53); drain and rinse; set aside same pot for cooking *Chili.*
4) **Thaw** and **crumble tofu** for *Chili* (#1, p. 54).
5) In large pot **saute vegetables** for *Chili* (#2, p. 54).
6) While *Chili* vegetables saute, begin to **saute vegetables** for *Chicken Hawaiian* in large fry pan (#2, p. 50).

COMPLETE CASSEROLES

1) Add remaining *Chili* ingredients to large pot and complete cooking (#2, 3, p. 54).
2) Complete *Chicken Hawaiian* from #3, p. 50; place in freezer container; rinse pan for *Noodle Parmesan.*
3) Place *Chili* in freezer container; rinse pot.
4) Prepare *Autumn Stew* in same pot from #2, p. 52.
5) While *Autumn Stew* cooks, complete **Noodle Parmesan** in large fry pan from #2, p. 53; place in freezer container; rinse pan for *Meatballs.*
6) Make *Meat Balls* in same pan from #1, p. 51.
7) Complete placing casseroles in **freezer containers**, label with names, date and desired cooking/serving instructions.
8) **Cool** completely in refrigerator; **freeze.**

Chicken Hawaiian

Serve over chow mein noodles and/or brown rice. Freeze a recipe of **Brown Rice** *separately or use quick brown rice (p. 65). For delicious menu, see p. 47.*

AMOUNT: 4 to 6 Servings (Approximately 2 qt. casserole)

1. Cook chicken *(p. 21)*, reserving any broth for another use:
   1 lb. boneless, skinned chicken breast, (2 cups) cut into small chunks before cooking

2. Saute vegetables in oil until just crisp-tender, about 4 minutes:
   1 tablespoon olive oil
   2 cups celery, sliced thinly on diagonal
   1 medium onion, sliced and separated into rings

3. To make **sweet 'n sour sauce** blend together in small bowl, stir into vegetables and cook and stir until thickened over medium heat:
   1 cup pineapple juice, drained from pineapple chunks chunks *(#4 below)* + water as needed to make 1 cup
   1/3 cup apple cider vinegar
   1/4 cup honey
   2 tablespoons soy sauce
   2 tablespoons cornstarch or arrowroot powder
   1/2 teaspoon ginger

4. Remove from heat and fold in:
   cooked chicken
   2 oz. jar pimineto, drained and chopped (or saute fresh red pepper strips the last minute or two with vegetables)
   20 oz. can pineapple chunks, unsweetened, drained
   1/2 cup roasted, unsalted cashews
   1/2 cup frozen green peas, unthawed and broken up

5. Freeze cooled casserole. To thaw and reheat see pp. 12-13.

Per serving of 6
   Exchanges: 2 Meat, 2 Fat, 1 Bread, 1.5 Fruit, 1 Vegetable
   349 Calories
   30 gm. protein (29%), 10 gm. fat (25%), 40.5 gm. carbohydrate (46%)
   4.5 gm. dietary fiber
   58 mg. cholesterol, 304 gm. sodium
   $1.25

 Extra Timesaver Tip: Plan menus, at least the evening meals for the week. It is less stress to prepare what your menu tells you to than trying to think up what to prepare on the day you must prepare it! Take advantage of our **Menu Planner** (order blank at back of book).

Little Saucy Meat Balls

*Serve over mashed potatoes, whole grain toast, whole grain noodles, or brown rice. **Brown Rice** can be cooked ahead and frozen separately (pp. 8, 65). Enjoy a lowfat menu (25%) with vegetable and salad, p. 47.*

AMOUNT: 4 to 6 Servings

1. Make crumbs in blender using:
   **1 slice whole wheat bread, dry or toasted, torn into pieces
   about 1/2 bunch fresh parsley, stems removed**

2. Combine thoroughly in mixing bowl, shape mixture into 18 to 20 2" balls and brown on all sides in nonstick pan:
   **I lb. ground turkey
   bread crumb mixture
   1/3 cup chopped onion
   1/4 cup lowfat milk
   3/4 teaspoon salt
   1/2 teaspoon pepper
   1/4 teaspoon thyme
   1/4 teaspoon lemon peel** (bottled or fresh)

3. Add **1 cup water,** cover, and simmer 10 minutes.

4. Blend together and stir into pan with meat balls, bringing to a boil; cook and stir 1 minute to thicken lightly:
   **2 cups water
   2 tablespoons lemon juice
   2 tablespoons cornstarch or arrowroot powder
   1 teaspoon worcestershire sauce**

5. Cool and freeze. To thaw and reheat see pp. 12-13.

Per serving of 4
   Exchanges: 2.75 Meat, 0.5 Bread, 0.75 Vegetable
   225 Calories
   25.5 gm. protein (44%), 9 gm. fat (35%), 12.5 gm. carbohydrate (21%)
   3.5 gm. dietary fiber
   67 mg. cholesterol, 496 mg. sodium
   $.75

Extra Timesaver Tip: When planning the week's menus on paper, write the page number beside each recipe: i.e. *Little Saucy Meat Balls (p. C51)*. *"C "* means the recipe is from **Casseroles.** This saves the step of looking up the recipe in the index or recipe list when you start preparation. For reference, I use *MD* for **Main Dishes**, *SM* for **Soups & Muffins**, etc.

Autumn Stew

A very tasty soup-like stew! Sausage flavored ground turkey is delicious and replaces bacon of original recipe. This is the lowest calorie recipe in this book! Enjoy it with salad and whole grain bread (see lowest calorie menu on p. 47).

AMOUNT: 6 to 8 Servings (approximately 2 1/2 qt. casserole)

1. Combine turkey with seasonings and brown in ungreased fry pan breaking up turkey into fairly good sized chunks:

   1 lb. ground turkey
   1 teaspoon salt
   1/2 teaspoon nutmeg
   1/2 teaspoon thyme
   1/16 teaspoon cayenne pepper

2. Cut fresh vegetables in 2" pieces, combine in large pot and bring to a boil; lower heat, cover, and simmer 15 to 20 minutes:

   1 lb. yellow squash (such as peeled banana squash)
   1 lb. summer squash, seeded (patty pan, scallop, crookneck)
   1 small eggplant, peeled
   29 oz. can whole tomatoes (3 1/2 cups)

3. Add and simmer 15 minutes longer:

   browned turkey
   1/2 lb. fresh mushrooms, quartered
   1 green pepper, cut into medium pieces
   1 medium zucchini, unpeeled and sliced

4. Cool and freeze. To thaw and reheat see pp. 12-13.

5. To serve, season to taste with any of the following:

   Spike Seasoning
   garlic powder
   other favorite seasoning

Per serving of 8
(seasonings in #5 not included, see p. 71)
   Exchanges: 1.25 Meat, 0.25 Bread, 3 Vegetable
   176 Calories
   15 gm. protein (32%), 5 gm. fat (23%), 21 gm. carbohydrate (45%)
   5.5 gm. dietary fiber
   33 mg. cholesterol, 439 mg. sodium
   $.85

Extra Timesaver Tip: In addition to prepared greens for salads (p. 66), keep a tupperware container filled with other salad ingredients. Wash, dry, and store a fresh supply weekly. Include a couple carrots for slicing and grating into salads, radishes, a couple of celery sticks, a small zucchini and/or cucumber, cherry tomatoes, jicama, etc. This type storage avoids having to get several different packages out of different drawers and shelves just to make one salad!

Noodle Parmesan Supreme

AMOUNT: 4 to 5 Servings (approximately 2 qt. casserole)

1. To cook pasta, add noodles, salt, and oil to boiling water, boil 5 to 6 minutes just until barely tender, adding the broccoli and zucchini to noodles to cook the last minute; drain and rinse all in cold water:
   4 quarts boiling water
   1/4 teaspoon salt
   1 teaspoon olive oil
   8 oz. whole grain noodles
   1 cup broccoli flowers
   1 cup chopped, unpeeled zucchini (1 small)

2. Saute almonds and garlic in butter:
   1/2 stick (1/4 cup) unsalted butter, melted
   1/4 cup almonds, slivered or chopped
   2 cloves garlic, minced

3. Blend together and stir into almonds:
   1 cup sour cream or light sour cream
   1/2 cup Parmesan cheese
   1/2 teaspoon salt, to taste

4. Fold in drained noodles and vegetables.

5. Cool and freeze. To thaw and reheat see pp. 12-13.

6. To serve, spark up the color with garnish of **parsley.**

Per serving of 5 (with sour cream)
   Exchanges: 0.75 Meat, 5 Fat, 2.25 Bread, 0.5 Vegetable
   443 Calories
   15 gm. protein (13%), 27 gm. fat (54%), 38 gm. carbohydrate (33%)
   11 gm. dietary fiber
   53 mg. cholesterol, 561 mg. sodium
   $.75

Per serving of of 5 (with light sour cream)
   Exchanges: 0.75 Meat, 4.5 Fat, 2.25 Bread, 0.5 Vegetable
   416 Calories
   16 gm. protein (15%), 22.5 gm. fat (48%), 39 gm. carbohydrate (37%)
   11 gm. dietary fiber
   49 mg. cholesterol, 577 mg. sodium
   $.75

 Extra Timesaver Tip: Keep 4 to 6 hard-cooked eggs on hand to garnish salads with minced egg, wedges, or slices. Keep them in the egg box. Place a pencil mark on top to distinguish them from the raw eggs.

Chili Gourmet

*Different and delicious with tofu! Freezing tofu completely changes the texture. An experiment to omit step #1 below and just freeze the tofu in the Chili afterwards did not achieve as good a result in the change of texture. If desired, substitute 1 lb. **Seasoned Ground Turkey** (p. 65) for the tofu. For menu see p. 47.*

AMOUNT: 6 to 8 Servings (10 cups or two 1 1/2 qt. casseroles)

1. To prepare tofu, drain block, cover with fresh water and freeze overnight. Thaw under running hot water, gradually pressing out the moisture and crumbling it as it thaws; set aside:
   14.2 oz. block tofu (or between 12 and 19 oz.)

2. Saute vegetables in a little water or olive oil (for added flavor); add tofu and remaining ingredients:
   1 onion, chopped
   1 large green pepper, chopped
   2 cups sliced fresh mushrooms
   15 oz. + 27 oz. cans kidney beans (50% salt reduced), drained and well rinsed *(see note, p. 46 and below)*
   1 1/2 cups water (or bean juice, if you prefer)
   2 1 lb. cans tomato pieces (4 cups)
   2 cloves garlic, minced or 1/4 teaspoon garlic powder
   1 tablespoon chili powder
   1 1/2 teaspoons cumin powder
   1 teaspoon salt, to taste

3. Add water, if needed to just cover ingredients, bring just to a boil, reduce to simmer and cook briefly, about 10 minutes.

4. Cool and freeze. To thaw and reheat, see pp. 12-13.

Per serving of 8
(olive oil for sauteeing not included, see p. 71)
  Exchanges: 1.25 Meat, 1.75 Bread, 2.5 Vegetable
  265 Calories
  14.5 gm. protein (22%), 2.5 gm. fat (9%), 46 gm. carbohydrate (69%)
  13.5 gm. dietary fiber, 952 mg. sodium
  $1.00

Note: If you prefer to use dry beans, cover **2 cups dry kidney beans** with **6 cups water** in crock-pot and cook on low overnight or until tender; drain before you add remaining ingredients. Two other ways to cook the dry beans are by pressure cooking (see note on p. 30) or on stove top (#1, 2, p. 30). To reduce the gas producing property of beans, soak before cooking, change to fresh water, if desired, and add a couple teaspoons garlic powder to the cooking water.

Menus

Chicken Tetrazzini
Fresh or Frozen Green Beans
Mid East Spinach Salad
(Main Dishes, p. 244)
Buttermilk Biscuits (p. 70)
w/Jam

$1.65
30% Fat
786 Calories

Barbecued Beans 'n Franks
Tossed Salad
w/Herb Vinegar
Minute Bran Muffins
(Soups & Muffins, p. 61)
w/Jam
Pineapple Wedges

$2.25
26% Fat
914 Calories

Enchilada Casserole
Brown Rice (p. 65)
Carrot Zucchini Salad
(Main Dishes, p. 240)
w/Herb Vinegar
Apple & Orange Wedges

$1.70
31% Fat
623 Calories

Chicken Pilaf en Casserole
One Minute Broccoli (p. 66)
Holiday Cranberry Mold
on Greens
(Main Dishes, p. 251)
Blueberry Muffins (p. 69)
w/Whipped Butter

$1.95
19% Fat
811 Calories

Salmon a la Broccoli
Cooked Carrots
Sliced Tomatoes w/Sweet Basil
on Greens
w/Herb Vinegar
Orange Muffins (p. 69)

$1.90
24% Fat
748 Calories

Savory Spaghetti Squash
Tossed Salad
w/Avocado & Tomato
w/Herb Vinegar
Baked Brown Bread
(Main Dishes, p. 219)
w/Jam

$1.40
19% Fat
656 Calories

Ready·to·Serve Shopping List

Meats:
3 lbs. boneless chicken breast
1 lb. ground turkey
10 oz. package chicken weiners*

Dairy:
1 1/3 cups lowfat milk
3 cups nonfat milk
3/4 lb. butter
6 oz. cheddar cheese (1 1/2 cups)
5 oz. Parmesan cheese
    (or 5/8 cup)

Grains/Beans/Pasta/Nuts
1 lb. long grain brown rice
10 oz. whole grain spaghetti*
1/2 doz. stoneground corn tortillas*
1/4 cup slivered almonds
1/4 cup pine nuts* or
    slivered almonds

Staples/Seasonings/Spices:
Check **Basic Stock List**, p. 6
against recipes.

Canned Foods/Misc:
16 oz. enchilada or pasta sauce
    (2 cups)
2 4 oz. cans mushroom
    stems & pieces
2 1/4 oz. can sliced ripe olives
4 oz. can diced green chiles
8 oz. can sliced water chestnuts
4 oz. chow mein noodles (2 cups)
15 oz. can salmon
2 oz. white grape juice or
    cooking sherry (1/4 cup)
16 oz. box tofu, firm or regular
48 oz. chicken broth (optional,
    see #1 below)

Fresh Produce:
2 onions
1 green onion (optional, see 4., p. 59)
1/8–1/4 bunch celery (or 2 stalks)
1 large or 2 medium carrots
1 medium spaghetti squash
1 medium or 2 small zucchini
1 1/2 lbs. broccoli

Frozen:
10 oz. frozen cut green beans
10 oz. frozen green lima beans
10 oz. frozen corn

*It may be necessary to purchase these items at a health food store.

Ready·to·Serve Assembly

NIGHT BEFORE

1) **Cook** and **refrigerate chicken** and **broth**
   for *Chicken Pilaf* and *Tetrazzini* (#1, pp. 58, 59).
2) Prepare **Yaki Tori Tofu** (p. 62) for *Savory Spaghetti Squash.*
3) **Freeze tortillas** for *Enchilada Casserole* (p. 62).
4) **Set out canned/dry ingredients,** grouping items for each
   recipe together.

NIGHT BEFORE, Con'd

6) **Get out freezer containers and cooking pans** (1 large fry pan, 1 large pot for cooking pasta, large saucepan for *Pilaf,* 2 medium saucepans for rice, cheese sauce, and *Tetrazzini* sauce, large mixing bowl for *Spaghetti Squash*).

COOKING DAY

1) **Start *Brown Rice*** for *Salmon a la Broccoli* (#1, p. 29).
2) **Start rice** for *Chicken Pilaf* (#2, 3, p. 59).
3) **Cook spaghetti** for *Tetrazzini* (#2, p. 58); drain, rinse.
4) **Cook spaghetti squash** (#1, p. 63).
5) **Chop/slice/grate** and place in separate bowls, as needed:
   a) **onions:** chop 2 (pp. 60, 62); chop 1-2 green, (optional, see #4, p. 53).
   b) **celery:** dice 2 stalks (p. 63)
   c) **broccoli:** 1 1/2 lbs. cut in small flowers and chopped stalks (p. 61)
   d) **carrots:** grate 1 large or 2 medium (p. 63)
   e) **zucchini**, unpeeled: grate 2 small or 1 medium (p. 63)
   f) **cheese:** grate 1 1/2 cups (p. 62)
6) **Cook broccoli** (p. 66) for *Salmon a la Broccoli* (p. 61).
7) **Precook frozen vegetables** for *Barbecued Beans* (#1, p. 60).
8) **Remove spaghetti strings** from cooked squash (#2, p. 63).

COMPLETE CASSEROLES

1) Complete **Spaghetti Squash** from #3, p. 63 using large fry pan; wipe out pan for *Barbecued Beans.*
2) Complete **Barbecued Beans** from #2, p. 60 using same fry pan; place in freezer container; wipe or rinse out pan to brown turkey for *Enchilada Casserole.*
3) Complete **Enchilada Casserole** from #1, p. 62 using same fry pan to brown turkey and onion.
4) Complete **Chicken Pilaf** from #4, p. 59.
5) Complete **Chicken Tetrazzini** from #3, p. 58. Rinse out saucepan for *Creamy Salmon* cheese sauce.
6) Complete **Creamy Salmon a la Broccoli** from #2, p. 61 using same pan for sauce as for *Tetrazzini* sauce.
7) Complete placing casseroles in **freezer containers,** label with names, date, and desired cooking/serving instructions.
8) **Cool** completely in refrigerator; **freeze.**

Chicken Tetrazzini

AMOUNT: 6 to 8 Servings (2 qt. to 2 1/2 qt. casserole)

1. Prepare chicken and chicken broth *(pp. 21-22)*:
   1 1/2 lbs. boneless chicken breast (3 cups)
   (skinned, fat removed)

2. To cook pasta, add spaghetti, salt, and oil to boiling water and cook just until barely tender, 7 to 10 minutes; drain and rinse in cold water:
   4 quarts boiling water
   1/4 teaspoon salt
   1 teaspoon oil
   10 oz. whole grain spaghetti

3. To make the **sauce**, blend flour into butter; cook and stir over medium heat about 1 minute; remove from heat and blend in milk and chicken broth. Return to heat; cook and stir until thickened; blend in remaining ingredients:
   1 stick (1/2 cup) melted butter, unsalted (half may be oil)
   1/2 cup whole wheat pastry flour (preferred)
   (or 6 Tablespoons unbleached white flour)
   1 3/4 cups hot lowfat milk
   1 cup hot chicken broth (fat removed)
   1/4 cup white grape juice or dry cooking sherry
   1/2 teaspoon salt
   1/4 teaspoon pepper
   1/8 teaspoon nutmeg
   4 oz. can mushroom stems & pieces, drained

4. Combine spaghetti, chicken, and sauce and place in casserole dish. Top with:
   1/3 cup Parmesan cheese

5. Cool and freeze. To thaw and reheat, see pp. 12-13.

Per serving of 8 (using 1/4 cup each oil and butter in #3)
   Exchanges: 2.5 Meat, 0.25 Milk, 2.5 Fat, 2.25 Bread, 0.25 Vegetable
   463 Calories
   34 gm. protein (30%), 18.5 gm. fat (36%), 36.5 gm. carbohydrate (32%)
   1.5 gm. dietary fiber
   88 mg. cholesterol, 454 mg. sodium
   $1.15

The wise woman builds her house, but with her own hands the foolish one tears hers down. Proverbs 14:1 (NIV)

Chicken Pilaf en Casserole

This recipe is especially tasty with **Sue's "Kitchen Magic" Seasoning** *(p. 18). See* **Variation** *below.*

AMOUNT: 6 Servings (9 x 13" pan or 2 1/2 qt. casserole)

1. Prepare chicken and chicken broth *(pp. 21-22)*; chop into bite sized pieces:

    1 lb. boneless chicken breast (2 cups) (skinned, fat removed)

2. Lightly brown the rice and almonds in butter (optional for flavor):

    1/4 cup unsalted butter, melted
    1 1/2 cups long grain brown rice, uncooked
    1/4 cup almonds, slivered

3. Combine liquid ingredients, bring to a boil, stir in rice and almonds; boil uncovered 5 minutes; cover tightly with lid, reduce heat to low and simmer 40 to 60 minutes until all the water is absorbed and rice is just barely tender:

    3 cups chicken broth (fat removed)
    1/2 teaspoon salt (omit if broth is salted)
    1/8 teaspoon garlic powder

4. Fold into cooked rice:

    8 oz. can sliced water chestnuts, drained
    4 oz. can mushroom stems and pieces, drained
    cooked chicken
    1 or 2 green onions, chopped (these may be added just before serving, if desired, either raw or lightly sauteed)

5. Cool and freeze. To thaw and reheat see pp. 12-13. If needed add a little extra water to moisten casserole.

Per serving of 6
(butter for sauteeing in #2 not included, see p. 71)
   Exchanges: 2 Meat, 0.75 Fat, 2.5 Bread, 0.75 Vegetable
   342 Calories
   28 gm. protein (33%), 6.5 gm. fat (18%), 42 gm. carbohydrate (49%)
   4 gm. dietary fiber
   58 mg. cholesterol, 452 mg. sodium
   $1.05

VARIATION
   In place of chicken broth use:
      3 cups water
      4 teaspoons *Sue's "Kitchen Magic" Seasoning*
      2 teaspoons worcestershire sauce or soy sauce

Barbecued Franks 'n Beans

Compare the fat percentage of this recipe with the menu on p. 55. Sodium level of this recipe is very high. Most of the sodium is in the weiners (616 mg. per frank). For variation, consider using 1/2 package of weiners.

AMOUNT: 4 to 5 Servings (1 1/2 qt. casserole)

1. Precook vegetables in microwave or on range top according to package directions:

   10 oz. package cut frozen green beans (2 cups)
   10 oz. package frozen green lima beans (2 cups)
   10 oz. package frozen corn (2 cups)

2. Cut franks or weiners diagonally in bite sized pieces and brown lightly and evenly in butter; remove from pan:

   10 oz. package chicken weiners (Health Valley available in many health food stores is an excellent brand)
   2 tablespoons olive oil   or unsalted butter, melted

3. Saute onion in same pan, adding a little more fat, if needed, or water (onion may also be sauteed in a little water in the micro-wave), and blend in remaining ingredients; simmer for 15 minutes:

   1 onion, chopped
   1/2 cup water
   1/2 cup ketsup, no salt added *(p. 19)*
   1/4 cup apple cider vinegar
   1 tablespoon honey or crystalline fructose
   1 tablespoon worcestershire sauce
   1 teaspoon dry mustard, no salt added *(see Note, p. 34)*
   1 teaspoon salt
   1 teaspoon paprika
   1/2 teaspoon pepper
   1/4 teaspoon Tabasco sauce

4. Combine vegetables, franks, and sauce in casserole dish. Cool and freeze.

5. To thaw and reheat see pp. 12–13. If microwaving thawed casserole, stir at least once half way through and again before serving.

6. Good served with yogurt, sour cream, or a blend of both.

Per serving of 5 (using olive oil in #2)
   Exchanges: 1.25 Meat, 5 Fat, 1.5 Bread, 1.5 Vegetable
   450 Calories
   19 gm. protein (16%), 24 gm. fat (46%), 45 gm. carbohydrate (38%)
   9 gm. dietary fiber
   90 mg. cholesterol, 1756 mg. sodium
   $1.40

Salmon a la Broccoli

Enjoy the benefits of salmon in tasty cheese sauce in a lowfat menu (24%), p. 55.

AMOUNT: 6 Servings (2 qt. casserole)

1. Prepare 2 cups **Brown Rice** *(p. 65)* using **1 1/3 cups water, 1/2 teaspoon salt,** and **2/3 cup uncooked brown rice.**

2. Place cooked rice in bottom of casserole dish and layer over top:

   1 1/2 lb. broccoli, cooked *(p. 66)*, **cut in small flowers and chopped, peeled stalks**

   15-16 oz. can (2 cups) salmon, drained (crumbled between fingers including the soft bones, an excellent calcium source)

   2 teaspoons lemon juice

3. To make **cheese sauce,** blend flour into butter over medium heat, stirring and cooking about 1 minute; remove from heat and gradually blend in milk so that no lumps remain. Return to heat and cook and stir until thickened; blend in cheese and seasonings:

   1/4 cup melted butter, unsalted (or 2 tablespoons each butter and oil)

   5 tablespoons whole wheat pastry flour (preferred) (or 1/4 cup unbleached white flour)

   3 cups nonfat or lowfat milk

   1/4 cup Parmesan cheese

   3/4 teaspoon dry mustard

   3/16 teaspoon cayenne pepper, to taste

   1/8 scant teaspoon nutmeg

4. Pour sauce over all and top with:

   1/4 cup pine nuts or slivered almonds

5. Cool and freeze. To thaw and reheat see pp. 12-13.

Per serving of 6
(with half oil and butter and nonfat milk in sauce)
   Exchanges: 2 Meat, 0.5 Milk, 2.25 Fat, 1.5 Bread, 1 Vegetable
   390 Calories
   26 gm. protein (26%), 18 gm. fat (41%), 33 gm. carbohydrate (33%)
   4.5 gm. dietary fiber
   44 mg. cholesterol, 714 mg. sodium
   $1.15

Jesus came, took the bread and gave it to them, and did the same with the fish. John 21:13 (NIV)

Enchilada Casserole

Tortillas tend to become soft and break up easily when frozen with sauce. To minimize this, freeze the tortillas before preparing the casserole. Assemble with frozen tortillas, thawing only enough so that they can be separated without breaking.

AMOUNT: 4 to 5 Servings (2 qt. casserole)

1. Brown in fry pan:
   1 lb. *Seasoned Ground Turkey* *(p. 65)*
   1 small onion, chopped

2. Layer alternately in casserole dish beginning and ending with sauce:
   2 cups pasta or enchilada sauce
   6 stoneground corn tortillas
   1 1/2 cups grated cheddar cheese
   2 1/4 oz. can sliced ripe olives, drained
   4 oz. can diced green chiles

3. Freeze casserole immediately. To thaw and reheat see pp. 12–13. While reheating you may want to add more enchilada sauce.

Per serving of 5
    Exchanges: 2 Meat, 4..25 Fat, 1 Bread, 2.5 Vegetable
    432 Calories
    31 gm. protein (28%), 21 gm. fat (43%), 33 gm. carbohydrate (29%)
    6.5 gm. dietary fiber
    88 mg. cholesterol, 675 mg. sodium
    $1.30

Yaki Tori Tofu

*Use this recipe for **Savory Spaghetti Squash** (p. 63).*

1. Drain block of tofu on a plate between paper towels for at least 30 minutes; cut into small cubes and marinate overnight or several hours in combined remaining ingredients:
   16 oz. box tofu, regular or firm
   1/2 cup soy sauce
   3 tablespoons lemon juice
   2 teaspoons honey or crystalline fructose
   1 teaspoon ginger
   1/8 teaspoon garlic powder

Savory Spaghetti Squash

*This recipe is unusual and very healthful. Since it will be new to the tastes of many, we have included **Chicken Tetrazzini** in this set of casseroles as an alternative. But do give this one a good try!*

AMOUNT: 6 to 8 Servings (freeze in 2 shell halves)

1. To cook squash, halve a medium **spaghetti squash**, remove seeds, place half the squash cut side up in shallow dish, add **1/4 cup water,** cover lightly with plastic wrap, and microwave for 7–8 minutes; repeat with second half (or boil whole, covered with water 20 to 30 minutes, or bake at 400º about 1 hour; halve and remove seeds). Cool a little.

2. Hold each squash half with pot holder and run a fork around sides of cooked squash and pull out the spaghetti strings into a large mixing bowl; reserve the shells.

3. Saute vegetables in melted butter briefly and combine with remaining ingredients and spaghetti squash strings:

   3 tablespoons melted butter
   1 large carrot, grated
   2 small or 1 medium zucchini, unpeeled and grated
   2 stalks celery, diced
   Yaki Tori Tofu *(p. 62)*, **drained** (don't worry if tofu cubes break up while combining ingredients)
   1/2 teaspoon salt
   1/4 teaspoon garlic powder
   1/4 teaspoon pepper

4. Pile mixture into squash shell halves. Cover securely with plastic wrap, then foil. Cool and freeze.

5. To thaw and reheat, see pp. 12–13.

6. Just before serving top each spaghetti squash half with noodles and fold in:
   1 cup chow mein noodles per half (optional)

Per serving of 8 (chow mein noodles excluded)
Exchanges: 0.5 Meat, 0.75 Fat, 0.25 Bread, 3 Vegetable
144 Calories, 7 gm. protein (20%), 6 gm. fat (38%), 15.5 gm. carbohydrate (42%)
4 gm. dietary fiber, 12 mg. cholesterol, 761 mg. sodium
$.60

Per serving of 8 (with chow mein noodles)
Exchanges: 0.5 Meat, 0.75 Fat, 1.25 Bread, 3 Vegetable
211 Calories, 9 gm. protein (17%), 9 gm. fat (37%), 24.5 gm. carbohydrate (46%)
4.5 gm. dietary fiber, 12 mg. cholesterol, 868 mg. sodium
$.65

Parmesan Chicken Mix

This is one of our favorite ways to prepare chicken and most frequent way prepared for company and special occasions.

AMOUNT: Coats 8–10 lbs. boneless chicken (24 Servings)

1. Blend into a crumb mixture in blender; store in a tightly closed labeled container in the freezer:
   4 slices soft whole wheat bread (4 cups crumbs)
   1/4 cup dry parsley flakes
   3/4 cup to 2 cups Parmesan cheese (3/4 cup for lowfat)
   1/2 teaspoon garlic powder
   1/2 teaspoon salt
2. Dip skinned chicken pieces into **melted butter** or **nonfat milk** (for lowfat version); coat with **crumb mixture**. Single layer in buttered or sprayed baking dish; garnish with **paprika**. Microwave, (or bake uncovered at 350° until tender, about 1 hour, basting a time or two during cooking; cover with foil if top gets too brown before it is done).

Per serving of 24 (crumb mixture only for 5 to 6 oz. serving chicken; 3/4 cup cheese in recipe)
   Exchanges: 0.25 Meat, 0.25 Bread
   29 Calories
   2 gm. protein (26%), 1 gm. fat (34%), 3 gm. carbohydrate (40%)
   0.5 gm. dietary fiber, 2 mg. cholesterol, 107 mg. sodium
   $.05

Fish Breading Mix

Our favorite way to prepare most fish!

AMOUNT: About 2 5/8 Cups (21 Servings)

1. Blend altogether and store in tightly closed labeled container in freezer:
   1 cup dry whole wheat bread crumbs (1 slice in blender)
   1 cup stoneground cornmeal
   1/2 cup toasted wheat germ
   1/2 cup Parmesan cheese
   1 to 2 teaspoons salt
   1 teaspoon paprika
2. To prepare fish, dip pieces in **melted butter** or **nonfat milk** and coat with **crumb mixture**. Microwave (or bake uncovered at 400° until it flakes easily, 20 to 30 minutes).

Per 2 tablespoons (crumb mixture only using 1 teaspoon salt in #1)
   Exchanges: 0.25 Meat, 0.5 Bread
   47 Calories
   2.5 gm. protein (22%), 1.5 gm. fat (25%), 6.5 gm. carbohydrate (53%)
   1.5 gm. dietary fiber, 2 mg. cholesterol, 147 mg. sodium
   $.05

Seasoned Ground Turkey

Great in any recipe calling for hamburger or ground beef; seasoning improves flavor.

Blend together before browning:
1 lb. ground turkey
1/2 teaspoon *Ground Turkey Seasoning Mix* (below)
1 tablespoon soy sauce
2 tablespoons ketsup, no salt added (p. 19)

Per 1b. (using Turkey Store brand, see p. 20)
Exchanges: 11 meat; 668 Calories, 92 gm. protein (53%), 33 gm. fat (43%),
262 mg. cholesterol, 6.5 gm. carbohydrate (4%), 0.5 gm. dietary fiber, 400 mg. sodium,
$2.75

Ground Turkey Seasoning Mix

AMOUNT: Seasons 48 lbs. of ground turkey

Blend together thoroughly and store in tightly covered labeled container in kitchen cupboard.
Use **1/2 teaspoon** per 1 lb. ground turkey:
2 tablespoons nutmeg
2 tablespoons thyme
2 tablespoons garlic powder
2 tablespoons sage

Brown Rice

To freeze, and reheat thawed brown rice see p. 8.
AMOUNT: 4 to 6 Servings (3 cups)

1. Place in saucepan and bring to a boil; boil uncovered for 5 minutes:
   2 to 2 1/2 cups water
   1 cup brown rice, washed
   1 teaspon salt (optional for best flavor)

2. Lower heat to very low, cover tightly, and simmer 45 to 60 minutes until water is absorbed and grain is tender.

Per 1/2 cup (long grain, with salt, see p. 71)
Exchanges: 1.5 Bread; 11 Calories, 2.5 gm. protein (8%), 0.5 gm. fat (5%),
24 gm. carbohydrate (87%), 2.5 gm. dietary fiber, 359 mg. sodium, $.05

Quick Brown Rice

Follow package directions for conventional or microwave cooking. Either will cook in about 14 minutes. Quick brown rice is not suited to freezing.

Five Minute Salad

The secret to quick fresh salads are salad greens that are already washed and dry. Do this one step in advance and you will save a lot of last minute time! You can prepare an 8-vegetable tossed salad in 5 minutes this way. Greens will stay fresh for the week.

1. Fill the sink with cool water *(see Note below)*.

2. Pull salad green leaves (**dark leafy green lettuce** for extra vitamin A) off the head and drop into water, swish around well and lift immediately out of the water to drain in a colander.

3. Fill sink with plain water and rinse again. Check for bugs and dirt in the water; rinse a third time, if necessary.

4. Put greens in a langerie bag (purchased at a department or variety store), fasten at the top and spin the water out in your automatic washing machine on the last spin cycle, 1 minute.

   Sue's langerie bag (under $5) has outlasted 3 $14-salad spinners. The trip to and from the washing machine is harmless good exercise!

5. Line a large tupperware mixing bowl or plastic bag with piece of paper towel, add the greens, top with another piece of paper towel; close tupperware bowl tightly or plastic bag loosely and refrigerate.

Note: In our first edition we recommended adding vinegar to the water to help remove some of the surface pesticide. We have found this not to be effective. Liquid *Castile* soap, available in health food stores, may be used. If you use it, you will need to rinse every lettuce leaf separately and very carefully to remove the soap!

One Minute Broccoli

What vegetable will provide you with the vitamin C of 4 oranges, the calcium of a cup of cottage cheese, the potassium of 2 bananas and the vitamin A of almost a dozen eggs and 8 grams of protein? Just a 73 calorie 1/2 lb. stalk of fresh broccoli! Here is a fool-proof and fast way to keep it beautifully green and not overcooked!

1. Trim and cut broccoli as desired.

2. Bring enough water to cover the broccoli to a boil; add broccoli, cover with a lid and boil 40 to 60 seconds (Yes, that's all!). Drain immediately.

3. If you prefer to steam it, steam for 5 minutes only.

Cornbread Mix

AMOUNT: Approximately 10 Cups (four 8" or 9" square pans)

1. Blend together thoroughly, sifting or stirring through a strainer to break of any lumps:

   4 cups stoneground cornmeal
   4 cups whole wheat flour (pastry preferred),
   or 4 more cups stoneground cornmeal
   1 cup crystalline fructose *(p. 17)*
      or use honey later *(see Note below)*
   1 cup cultured buttermilk blend or powder *(p. 16)*
   3 tablespoons baking powder *(low sodium preferred, p. 16)*
   4 teaspoons salt

2. Store in tightly covered container or divide 4 equal portions of about 2 1/2 cups each into ziploc bags (6 1/2" x 5 7/8").

3. Freeze or refrigerate. For best results bring mix to room temperature before using in recipe.

Note: **3 tablespoons honey** (or maple syrup) can be blended with the eggs in recipe below in place of fructose, if desired.

Cornbread

AMOUNT: 8" or 9" Square Bake Pan (16 pieces)
Oven: 350°   *Bake: 25–30 minutes*

Blend ingredients together in order given just until moistened; pour into greased 8" or 9" pan and bake at 350° for 25–30 minutes:

   2 eggs, beaten
   1/2 stick (1/4 cup) butter, melted
   1 cup water
   1 portion (about 2 1/2 cups) *Cornbread Mix,* **room temperature**

Per piece (16 per pan; with low sodium baking powder)
Exchanges: 0.125 Meat, 0.75 Fat, 1 Bread; 118 Calories, 3 gm. protein (9%), 5 gm. fat (35%), 17 gm. carbohydrate (56%), 2 gm. dietary fiber, 28 mg. cholesterol, 151 mg. sodium, $.10

Pineapple Corn Muffins

AMOUNT: 12 Muffins
Oven: 350°   *Bake: 20 minutes*

Follow *Cornbread* recipe using **8 oz can crushed unsweetened pineapple** in place of the water. Fill greased or paper-lined muffin cups.

Per muffin (with low sodium baking powder)
Exchanges: 0.25 Meat, 0.125 Milk, 1 Fat, 1.25 Bread, 0.25 Fruit; 168 Calories, 4 gm. protein (9%), 6.5 gm. fat (33%), 26 gm. carbohydrate (58%), 3 gm. dietary fiber, 37 mg. cholesterol, 201 mg. sodium, $.15

Quick Muffin Mix

*Mix up delicious **Blueberry, Banana Nut, Orange, or Apple Raisin Muffins** with this easy muffin mix!*

AMOUNT: Approximately 10 1/2 Cups (Makes 48 muffins)

1. Blend together thoroughly by sifting or stirring through a large strainer to break up any lumps:

    8 cups whole wheat flour (pastry preferred)
    2 cups crystalline fructose *(p. 17)*
       or add honey later *(see Note below)*
    1 cup cultured buttermilk blend or powder *(p. 16, Note below)*
    2 tablespoons baking powder *(low sodium preferred, p. 16)*
    4 teaspoons salt
    2 teaspoons baking soda

2. Store in refrigerator or freezer in tightly covered container or equally divide into smaller amounts, as desired, and store in 6 1/2" x 5 7/8" ziploc bags:

    for 6 muffins: **scant 1 1/3 cups dry mix** (approximate)
    for 12 muffins: **scant 2 2/3 cups dry mix** (approximate)

3. For best results, bring mix to room temperature before preparing the muffins to bake. Cold ingredients will not allow the baking powder to act as effectively and muffins will not rise as well.

Note: If you desire, omit the fructose and blend honey with the eggs in muffin recipes following (p. 69). Use **1/3 to 1/2 cup honey** for 12 muffins, or **3 tablespoons to 1/4 cup honey** for 6 muffins. If you do not have buttermilk powder or cultured blend, use fresh buttermilk in place of water in same amount in the recipes that follow.

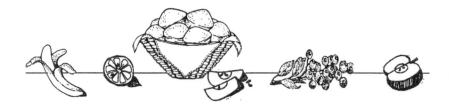

For the delicious muffins below blend ingredients together in order given just until thoroughly moist. Evenly fill greased or paper-lined muffin cups. Allow muffins in greased pan to cool 5 minutes or so before removing.

AMOUNT--All Recipes Below: 12 Muffins

Oven: 350°   *Bake: 20-25 minutes*

Blueberry Muffins

2 eggs, beaten
1 cup water
scant 2 2/3 cups *Quick Muffin Mix,* **room temperature**
1 cup fresh or frozen blueberries (rinse ice off of frozen berries)

Per muffin (with low sodium baking powder in muffin mix) Exchanges: 0.25 Meat, 1.75 Bread, 0.25 Fruit; 145 Calories, 4 gm. protein (11%), 1.5 gm. fat (10%), 31 gm. carbohyddrate (79%), 3 gm. dietary fiber, 37 mg. cholesterol, 236 mg. sodium, $.20

Banana Nut Muffins

1 egg, beaten
1/2 cup water
1 large banana, mashed (about 1/2 cup)
1/2 teaspoon cinnamon
1/2 cup chopped walnuts
scant 2 2/3 cups *Quick Muffin Mix,* **room temperature**

Per muffin (with low sodium baking powder in muffin mix) Exchanges: 0.75 Fat, 1.75 Bread, 0.25 Fruit; 173 Calories, 5 gm. protein (11%), 4 gm. fat (20%), 32 gm. carbohydrate (69%), 3 gm. dietary fiber, 19 mg. cholesterol, 231 mg. sodium, $.20

Orange Muffins

2 eggs, beaten
1/4 cup water
6 oz. can frozen orange juice concentrate, undiluted
scant 2 2/3 cups *Quick Muffin Mix,* **room temperature**
1 small orange, peeled and chopped

Per muffin (with low sodium baking powder in muffin mix) Exchanges: 0.25 Meat, 1.75 Bread, 0.75 Fruit; 171 Calories, 4.5 gm. protein (10%), 1.5 gm. fat (8%), 37 gm. carbohydrate (82%), 2.5 gm. dietary fiber, 37 mg. cholesterol, 236 mg. sodium, $.20

Apple Raisin Muffins

1 egg, beaten
1 cup water
1 1/2 teaspoons cinnamon
scant 2 2/3 cups *Quick Muffin Mix,* **room temperature**
1/2 cup raisins
1 medium apple, peeled or unpeeled, grated or chopped

Per muffin (with low sodium baking powder) Exchanges: 1.75 Bread, 0.75 Fruit; 157 Calories, 4 gm. protein (9%), 1 gm. fat (6%), 35.5 gm. carbohydrate (85%), 3 gm. dietary fiber, 19 mg. cholesterol, 232 mg. sodium, $.20

Buttermilk Biscuit Mix

AMOUNT: 10 1/2 to 11 Cups (makes about 48 biscuits)

1. Blend together thoroughly except the butter, sifting or stirring through a strainer to break up any lumps. With a pastry blender or two table knives cut in butter until crumbly (size of small peas):

   10 cups whole wheat flour (pastry preferred)
   3/4 cup cultured buttermilk blend or powder *(p. 16)*
   1/4 cup baking powder *(low sodium preferred, p. 16)*
   2 teaspoons salt
   2 sticks (1 cup) butter, cold, but not too hard

2. Store in sealed container or divide into 4 portions (2 1/2 to 3 cups each) and store in sealed ziploc bags (6 1/2" x 5 7/8"). Freeze or refrigerate.

Buttermilk Biscuits

AMOUNT: 12 Large Biscuits
Oven: 400°   *Bake: 10-15 minutes*

Blend ingredients together in order given just until moist. Knead lightly about 10 times on lightly floured board or pastry sheet. Pat dough out about 3/4" thick and cut with floured cookie cutter or rim of a glass; place on ungreased cookie sheet; bake at 400° for 10 to 15 minutes:

1 egg, beaten
3/4 cup water
1 portion (2 1/2 to 3 cups) Buttermilk Biscuit Mix, room temp.

Per biscuit (using low sodium baking powder)
   Exchanges: 0.125 Meat, 0.75 Fat, 1.5 Bread; 151 Calories, 4 gm. protein (10%), 5 gm. fat (28%), 25 gm. carbohydrate (62%), 3 gm. dietary fiber, 29 mg. cholesterol, 143 mg. sodium, $.10

Soup 'n Salad Croutons

AMOUNT: About 12 Cups
Oven: 300°   *Bake: 20-30 minutes*

Mix together well and bake in single layer on cookie sheet until crisp, about 20 to 30 minutes; cool and freeze in tightly closed ziploc bag:

1 1/2 lb. loaf whole grain bread, cubed
1 stick (1/2 cup) butter, melted
1/8 teaspoon garlic powder or 1 clove (mix with butter)
Spike Seasoning, to taste (or other favorite)

Per 1/4 cup (using 1/2 teaspoon Spike Seasoning in recipe):
   Exchanges: 0.5 Fat, 0.5 Bread; 51 Calories, 1.5 gm. protein (10%), 2.5 gm. fat (42%), 6.5 gm. carbohydrate (48%), 1 gm. dietary fiber, 5 mg. cholesterol, 101 mg. sodium, $.05

Using Fat & Salt

Many people believe that salt is best left out of recipes. The debate, however, continues. It has been found that of the 30% of the population in America who have high blood presssure only about half are salt-sensitive. This means that the blood pressure of 85% of the ¡population is unaffected by salt intake. For more information on salt read "A Salty Sermon," *Eating Right! pp. 115-117.*

Salt is essential for the savory flavor of many recipes. When used moderately, it does not exceed the safety limits for most people. In the *Eating Better Cookbooks* you may occasionally find recipes that seem high in sodium (see p. 60). The *Nutritional Goals Chart,* p. 73, will help put those recipes in perspective. Keep in mind that it is the average sodium intake of a period of time that counts.

In a few recipes fat or a high sodium seasoning is not included in the nutrient data (for example, see p. 59: *Per serving of 6 (butter for sauteeing in #2 not included, see p. 71).* The chart below will help you determine how these additions will affect the fat, cholesterol, and sodium content of a recipe.

Optional Ingredient	Amt.	Calo- ries	Fat*	Choles- terol	Sodium	Cost Est.
butter, salted	1 Tbsp.	100	12 gm.	31 mg.	116 mg.	.10
butter, unsalted	1 Tbsp.	100	12 gm.	31 mg.	neg.	.10
oil, canola	1 Tbsp.	120	14 gm.	0	0	.10
oil, olive	1 Tbsp.	125	14 gm.	0	0	.15
salt	1 tsp.	0	0	0	2132 mg.	.01
salt	3/4 tsp.	0	0	0	1599 mg.	neg.
salt	1/2 tsp.	0	0	0	1066 mg.	neg.
salt	1/4 tsp.	0	0	0	533 mg.	neg.
salt	1/8 tsp.	0	0	0	267 mg.	neg.
Spike Seasoning	1 tsp.	neg.	0	0	1066 mg. est.	.05
Sue's "Kitchen Magic" Seasoning	1 tsp.	10	0	0	710 mg.	.05

*1 gram fat = 9 calories

Nutritional Goals

The modern American averages a daily intake of 38–42% or more fat (of the total calories consumed), only 7 to 14 grams dietary fiber, and 10,000 to 15,000 milligrams sodium per day!

Contrast those figures to the 30% or less fat (of the total calories), 55% or more complex carbohydrates, 25 to 40 grams dietary fiber, and 1100 to 3300 milligrams sodium per day nutrient levels achieved using almost any combination of menus from the *Eating Better Cookbooks!*

The data below compiled from the 26 menus in this book demonstrates how these menus contribute to our daily nutritional goals.

GET PLENTY OF THESE (List not intended to be complete)	DAILY GOAL Amount	AVERAGE OF MAIN DISH MENUS	
		Amount	% of Daily Goal
COMPLEX CARBOHYDRATE	55 – 65% of Calories	55 – 57% of Calories	____
DIETARY FIBER	25 to 40 grams	25 gm.	83%
VITAMIN A	*RDA's: 5,000 I.U.	10,040 I.U.	200%
VITAMIN C	60 milligrams	83 mg.	138%
VITAMIN B-1 (Thiamine)	1.5 milligrams	0.7 mg.	47%
VITAMIN B-2 (Riboflavin)	1.7 milligrams	0.6-0.7 mg.	36–41%
VITAMIN B-3 (Niacin)	20 milligrams	11.2 mg.	56%
CALCIUM	1,000 milligrams	356 mg.	36%
POTASSIUM	3,750 milligrams	1,567 mg.	48%
IRON	15 milligrams	7.7 mg.	43%

*RDA's are for the "typical" adult (a "statistical" person).

Nutritional Goals

Our goal is to transform the typical American high fat-low fiber diet into a higher fiber-lower fat diet. By comparing the casserole menu averages with the daily nutritional goals for dietary fiber and fat, you can observe that these goals have been achieved. We encourage thinking in terms of entire menus over the nutrient value of single recipes, since it is the total of all food eaten that determines actual nutrient value.

Keep in mind that these figures are realistic--not the ideal projections of a "denial" or even a therapeutic diet--based on menus eaten over a period of time. Some menus in this book fall below and some above the percentage goals.

LIMIT THESE	DAILY GOAL	AVERAGE OF MAIN DISH MENUS
PROTEIN	10 - 15% of Calories	19% of Calories
FAT (TOTAL)	30% of Calories	26 - 27% of Calories
(Saturated fat)	(10% of Calories)	(9-10% of Calories)
(Monounsaturated fat)	(10% of Calories)	(11% of Calories)
(Polyunsaturated fat)	(10% of Calories)	(7% of Calories)
CHOLESTEROL	250-300 milligrams	100-102 milligrams
SODIUM	2200 milligrams (1100-3300mg)	1050-1060 milligrams
SUGAR	Reduce con- sumption by half (minimum goal)*	0.2 tsp.

*In 1988 the average per capita sugar consumption per year was about 130 lbs. per person, about 10 lbs. higher than in 1968. Artificial sweeteners have not curbed the average American sugar consumption. A recommended minimal reduction to 65 lbs. per year (reducing consumption by half) equals 6.5 Tbsp. granulated white sugar or 11 tsp. honey per day.

How to Read a Recipe

This cookbook is packed with information, some of it technical. However, the format is designed so the important items (e.g. ingredients and procedures) stand out from the details. The example below explains how the data and details relate to the recipe.

Nutrient data based on <u>first</u> listed ingredient, *(e.g. olive oil)* or <u>first amount</u> <u>listed</u> *(eg. 3 Tbsp. soy sauce)*

Exchange chart, p. 76; rounded to nearest 1/4 or 1/8 exchange

RECIPE SAMPLE
This recipe illustrates information you will want to understand; not a recipe to prepare and serve!
AMOUNT: Serves 4 to 6

1. Blend together:
   2 tablespoons olive oil or butter

   3–4 tablespoons soy sauce
   (Kikkoman Lite preferred, *p. 19*)

Per sering of 4
Exchanges: 1 Meat, 3.75 Bread, 1.5 Vegetable; 358 Calories, 20 gm. protein (21%), 2 gm. fat (5%), 68.5 gm. carbo- hydrate (74%), 15.5 gm. dietary fiber, 43 mg. sodium, $.40

Page where more information on product is given

Nutrient Data: fat, protein, carbohy- drate, fiber grams rounded to near- est 1/2 or whole.

Cost rounded off upward to nearest $.05; cost based on average food prices, So. CA, winter, 1989

NUTRIENT DATA SOURCES

Nutrient data for this book has been compiled from the following:

Nutrition Wizard, computer data program, Michael Jacobson, Center for Science in the Public Interest, 1986

Food Values of Portions Commonly Used, 14th Edition, Jean A.T. Pennington & Helen Nichols Church, Harper & Row, Publishers, 1985

Nutrition Almanac, Revised Edition, Nutrition Search, Inc., John D. Kirschmann, Director, McGraw-Hill Book Company, 1979

Composition of Foods, Agricultural Handbook #8, USDA, Washington, D.C., 1963

Laurel's Kitchen, Laurel Robertson, Carol Flinders & Bronwen Godfrey, Nilgiri Press, Berkeley, California, 1976

How to Read a Menu Box

26 Menus on pp. 23, 31, 39, 47, 55 accompany casserole recipes. Each menu box includes total cost, fat percentage, and calories for the complete menu in the box.

Country Creole Peas 'n Corn

Carrot & Celery Sticks,
Cucumber Slices
Minute Bran Muffins
(Soups & Muffins, p. 61)
w/Jam

$.80 – $.90
5% – 18% Fat
605 – 706 Calories

A few recipes include more than one total menu price, fat percentage, and calorie amount. This occurs when two sets of nutrient data are given for a casserole recipe for a particular variation. For example, in the menu above, *Country Creole Peas 'n Corn* may be prepared with or without the optional butter, and data reflecting this difference is presented at the end of the recipe *(see p. 37)*.

Menu cost, fat, and calories are based on the following:

Casserole recipe: 1 serving as given in the nutrient data information at the end of each recipe. For example, for *Country Creole Peas 'n Corn (p. 37):*

Per serving of 6 (without optional butter)
Exchanges: 0.75 Meat, 3 Bread, 2 Vegetable; 302 Calories, 16 gm. protein (21%), 1 gm. fat (3%), 60 gm. carbohydrate (76%), 12 gm. dietary fiber, 0 mg. cholesterol, 312 mg. sodium, $.45

Per serving of 6 (using optional butter)
Exchanges: 0.75 Meat, 2.25 Fat, 3 Bread, 2 Vegetable; 403 Calories, 16.5 gm. protein (16%), 12.5 gm. fat (27%), 12 gm. dietary fiber, 31 mg. cholesterol, 314 mg. sodium, $.55

Vegetable, Cooked: 1 cup broccoli or 1/2 cup other vegetable.
Salads: A typical portion size (most people eat about the same amount of certain kinds of salads) unless a specific recipe source is given. If specific salad recipe is listed, menu data is based on per serving data given for that recipe.
Breads, Muffins, Rolls, Biscuits: 1 1/2 slices or pieces unless otherwise listed.
Fruits, sliced: 3 slices orange, tomato; 2 slices pineapple, or about half piece fruit; 1/2 cup of seasonal fresh fruit
Raw Vegetables, Relish Tray: 1 cup; ave. serving carrot, celery sticks
Salad Dressing or Herb Vinegar: 1 tablespoon
Butter : 1 1/2 teaspoons unless otherwise listed.
Jam: 1 tablespoon

Using Food Exchanges

Several weight control programs use the food exchange system including Weight Watchers and The American Diabetes Association. If you are following one of these programs, you will appreciate the exchange values provided with every recipe in *Casseroles.*

If food exchanges are new to you, the following explanation will assist you in using the food exchange system for weight control. The chart below outlines the nutrient equivalents for food exchange values used in this book.

FOOD EXCHANGE VALUES*

	1 MEAT	1 MILK	1 FAT	1 BREAD	1 FRUIT	1 VEG.
CALORIES	60	95	45	70	40	25
Grams: PROTEIN	7	8	----	2.5	----	1.5
Grams: FAT	2-3	2	5	----	----	----
Grams: CARBOHYDRATE	----	11-12	----	15	10	5

*Food exchange values reflect averages of the variety of foods used in *Casseroles* and are a summary of the following sources:

> **Weight Watchers** (calorie levels only) (meat exchange is equivalent to protein exchange)
>
> *Controlling Cholesterol*, Dr. Kenneth H. Cooper, Bantam Books, 1988, p. 94.
>
> *Exchange Lists for Menu Planning*, American Diabetes Association, Inc., and The American Dietetic Association, 1986, pp. 5-21.
>
> *Eat and Stay Slim*, Better Homes and Gardens, New York, 1968, pp. 28-30.

SUMMARY GUIDE TO FOOD EXCHANGES

Meat: 60 Calories of meats, fish, poultry, cheeses, peanut butter, tofu, 1 cup cooked legumes, eggs

Milk: 95 Calories of milk, yogurt, kefir, dry milk, buttermilk, evaporated milk

Fat: 45 Calories of oils, butter, sour cream, cream cheese, avocados, nuts, seeds, olives, coconut, whipping cream, mayonnaise

Bread: 70 Calories of breads, cooked grains, cereals, green peas, potatoes, corn, legumes (minus 60 Calories per cup counted as meat exchange), winter squash, honey, fructose, jam, molasses, soy sauce

Fruit: 40 Calories all fruits and juices except those classified as fats

Vegetable: 25 Calories all vegetables except those classified as breads

Living Bread

I love working with food. I marvel at the variety, the textures, the flavors, the colors, and the endless ways to prepare it. There is almost nothing I like better than to serve others a beautiful satisfying meal of tasty, nutritious food. This interest was sparked in me even before I began a college career in home economics education.

But I had little awareness of the Master Chef, the personal Creator who had originated the foods I loved to prepare. My background wasn't religious, although from childhood I believed in my own idea of God. I had heard of Jesus, but I understood him only as the greatest man who ever lived. He was not essential to my belief in God. Yet, while my belief in God was a security, I had but a vague understanding of who he was. Thus my enrollment in college was just part of my own plan for fulfillment and had little to do with spiritual concernts.

When I began to attend a Bible study in my dormitory (under the pressure of much friendly persuasion), I brought my own idea of Jesus--the greatest man who ever lived. And that was all. I wasn't aware that He had created a complete meal for over 5,000 people out of 2 fish and 5 loaves of barley bread by just saying the word! I soon learned that my conception of him was far too limited.

In the beginning was the Word and the Word was with God, and the word was God...The Word became flesh and lived for a while among us. We have seen his glory, the glory of the one and only Son, who came from the Father, full of grace and truth. John 1:1, 14 (NIV)

Who was Jesus Christ? The greatest Man that ever lived? Yes! But much more. He was the living God! Was it possible that I could believe in God and reject Jesus Christ? No! *Through him all things were made; without him nothing was made that has been made. John 1:3* Jesus Christ was present and active in the creation of the world!

Why did I need to concern myself with believing in Jesus Christ? He sought a personal relationship with me. *My sheep listen to my voice I know them, and they follow me. John 10:27 (NIV)* He created food for me, but he created me for himself. And he designed me to live in a creature-creator relationship to himself, to honor and reflect his creative and moral magnificence.

Yet, there is a split between human beings and God which has been widening ever since Eve deliberately chose to defy his instructions by eating and serving the wrong food. She suffered the consequences of that choice--separation from his fellowship and death, both physical and spiritual. She chose to make her decisions about life independently of God, and that is exactly what I had done, too.

No one had ever explained to me that I was "spiritually dead" or that the purpose of God, the Son, *becoming flesh* was not just to identify with my human situation, although he did that, too. It was to accept the death penalty, to pay the price for human rebellion, that is human independence from God, and to restore the fellowship relationship. Imagine, the eternal, living, prsonal God taking my death sentence upon himself! Thus I discovered it is not possible to honor God or to know him without Jesus. I learned that receiving God, the Son, Jesus Christ, was receiving the Father as well. *I am the way and the truth and the life. No one comes to the Father except through me. If you really knew me, you would know my Father as well. From now on, you do know him and have seen him...Anyone who has seen me has seen the Father. John 14:6-7, 9 (NIV)*

I made a personal commitment of my life to Jesus Christ. *Yet to all who received him, to those who believed in his name, he gave the right to become children of God. John 1:12 (NIV)* It was a new beginning of forever living, not easy living, but living the way for which I was created.

Jesus said, "I am the bread of life. He who comes to me will never go hungry...I am the living bread that came down from heaven. If a man eats of this bread, he will live forever." John 6:35, 51 (NIV)

This is the living bread that you may eat of and not die.

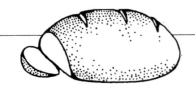

You can "Eat Better"
with Sue Gregg

Now frustrated homemakers regain confidence as Sue Gregg shares her secrets to eating better and pleasing family palates. Spend an hour with Sue and your whole life at the supermarket and in the kitchen will change.

After baby number four and a family health crisis, Sue began to question how to put nutritional value back into Betty Crocker style family meals. Nine months of endurance (although with positive results) on a rigorous, restrictive "healthfood" diet convinced her that few families would survive drastic dietary changes.

That motivated Sue to experiment with old recipes to see if it would be possible to retain familar tastes and textures with optimal nutritional quality. Others soon requested recipes and cooking classes. From those classes came the **Eating Better Cookbooks** and a demonstration video, *Eating Better with Sue*. Now she shares a teaching and publishing ministry with her husband, Rich. Sue Gregg also co-authored *Eating Right! A Realistic Approach to a Healthy Lifestyle* (Harvest, House) with Emilie Barnes to answer questions women repeatedly ask about food and feeding their families.

Is it possible to put nutrition back into old family favorites without getting yucks?

In an *Eating Right! Seminar* women benefit by learning how to enhance both nutritional value and appetite appeal. At the same time they discover how Sue's simple menu planning system saves time and money. In addition Sue's shows how to involve children in the learning process. She believes that healthy eating attitudes are modeled more by "doing" in the kitchen than by academic study.

Eating Right! Seminars apply biblical principles in evaluating commercial foods, popular diet trends, and New Age influences upon the healthfood industry. Sue Gregg does not dwell on the nutritional negatives of the typical diet. Instead, she offers acceptable alternatives aimed at turning yucks into yums.

Seminars are held throughout the country. They are sponsored by women's groups, home educators, MOPS, and health oriented business. Write or call for a national tour schedule and for information on organizing a seminar in your area.

Eating Right! Seminars
8830 Glencoe Drive, Riverside, California 92503 (714) 687-5491

Eating Better Cookbooks

COPIES

by Sue Gregg

___**Eating Right!** A Realistic Approach to a Healthy Lifestyle, $____

(Harvest House) Sue answers women's concerns about pleasing appetites, nutrition, resources, planning to save time and money. 287p. $9

COOKBOOKS

___**Main Dishes** Recipes & menus meet US dietary guidelines, 266p. $13 $____

___**Casseroles** Double recipes & freeze for convenience, 78p. $5 $____

___**Soups & Muffins** Low cost light & hearty recipes with menus, 92p. $6 $____

___**Lunches & Snacks** Kitchen & nutrition basics for children, 152p. $9 $____

___**Desserts** Sweets without white sugar or white flour, 104p. $6 $____

___**Breakfasts** New ideas to start your day, 82p. $5 $____

___The Six Cookbook Set: Over 700 recipes, Individually $44, Set $40 $____

> Set purchase includes 10 day viewing the **Eating Better with Sue** video.
> Models recipe basics. Motivates 8-12 year olds to get started .
> Enclose a separate refundable check for $20 marked "video deposit."

___**Sue's "Kitchen Magic" Seasoning** 8 oz $5. A blend of soy, $____

alfalfa, corn, and wheat. Flavors selected main dish, soup, and casserole Eating Better Cookbook recipes. Helps to reduce or omit salt. 24 oz $13

___**Menu Planners** Organizes to save time and costs. $5 $____

___**Holiday Menus** Celebrate in good taste and health 69p. $5 $____

___**Recipe Organizer** Don't loose another recipe! 200p. $5 $____

VIDEO COOKING COURSE

___**Eating Better with Sue** (90 minute VHS video) $20 $____

___10 day video rental including postage & handling $6 $____

Enclose a separate refundable check for $20 marked "video deposit."

___**Video Cooking Course Workbook** Seven lessons coordinate

video viewing with **Eating Right!** Guides children's kitchen activities. $4 $____

___All 13 above items (Individually $97) The Complete Works $80 $____

SUBTOTAL $____

Phone ( )_____   California residents add tax $____

U.S. Add 10% handling & shipping. For orders less than $20 add $2

Canadian residents add 15% H & S. For orders under $20 add $3 $____

Make check to: Eating Better Cookbooks (U.S. Funds Only)

TOTAL ENCLOSED $____

Eating Better Cookbooks   4th Class Books & Video
8830 Glencoe Drive
Riverside, CA 92503
(714) 687-5491

Name_____

Address_____

City_____ State____ Zip_____

Prices subject to change after 3/1/92. Write or call for current prices & order forms.

COOKBOOKS by Sue Gregg

Eating Right! A Realistic Approach to a Healthy Lifestyle answers questions about nutrition and food preparation. Tackles the obstacles to preparing wholefoods.

Main Dishes with over 200 recipes transforms the quality of familiar dishes. So versatile that it accommodates five monthly menu plans including unrestricted, low-fat, low-budget, and restricted vegetarian eating styles. Nutritional data includes food exchanges for weight watchers as well as costs for both recipes and menus.
Casseroles supplies shopping lists and assembly procedures for 25 dishes for freezing ready to pop in the oven or microwave when time and energy are short.
Soups & Muffins offers 36 whole grain muffin recipes and 27 favorite soup recipes revised for nutritional inprovement though quality ingredient selection. Alternative ingredients to dairy products and wheat for food allergies.
Lunches & Snacks teaches kids about preparing beverages, breads, crackers, chips, goodies, salads, sandwiches, soups, spreads, and dips. Includes quizzes on basic nutrition with answers. A home educator's must.
Breakfasts with fresh ideas for beverages, coffee cakes, pancakes and waffles, French toast, yeast breads, cereals, fruits, toppings and spreads.
Desserts without white sugar no longer a fantasy. Poppy Seed Cake and Sweet n' Spicy Pudding along with old favorites. 34 recipes under 200 Calories and 31% fat.

Holiday Menus provides recipes complete menus for Thanksgiving, Christmas, Passover Seder, Easter brunch, autumn harvest party, special company, yule luncheon and waffle bar. Celebrate in good taste and good health.

The Recipe Organizer saves you from the frustration of losing a collected recipe. Keep those "I want to try someday" recipes safely in a book of your own design.
Menu Planner keyed to **Eating Better Cookbooks.** Plan a month's menus in 20 minutes! Merge personal favorites with new *Eating Better* recipes. Two years of monthly planner pages color coded to seasons. Save time, frustration, and costs.

Have "More Hours In Your Day"
with Emilie Barnes

Energy, encouragement, and enthusiasm are what you get when you spend an hour with Emilie Barnes. Spend all morning with her and your home will be transformed. Spend all day with her and your whole life will be changed.

Emilie practices what she preaches and reaches those she teaches. Her bright eyes and bubbling personality captivate audiences and win friends wherever she goes. The reality of her life gives encouragement that you too will have more hours in your day.

More Hours in My Day is the cry of homemakers and working women everywhere and the title of Emilie's first book. Emilie married her husband Bob while she was a senior in high school. Three years later their first child was born and in six months Emilie was given her brother's three children to care for full time. As if that wasn't enough, the next year their second child was born. Emilie had five children under five and she was practically a child herself! She cried "I need *More Hours in My Day*!"

As Emilie got herself organized, she found time for herself, her husband, and her God. As a busy woman she survived. Thus was born the ministry of **MORE HOURS IN MY DAY.**

Much of Emilie's ministry is shared through her books, but her impact is even more powerful in person. She travels throughout the United States and Canada giving women guidance and hope that their lives can be "Super."

For order forms for Emilie's books or information on organizing a seminar write
More Hours in My Day 2838 Rumsey Drive, Riverside, CA 92506 (714) 682-4714